Language in Drama

Language in Drama

MEANINGS FOR THE DIRECTOR & THE ACTOR

WILLIAM L. SHARP
Emerson College

CHANDLER PUBLISHING COMPANY cp

An Intext Publisher · Scranton, Pennsylvania 18515

COPYRIGHT © 1970 BY CHANDLER PUBLISHING COMPANY
ALL RIGHTS RESERVED
INTERNATIONAL STANDARD BOOK NUMBER 0-8102-0014-7 (SOFT COVER)
INTERNATIONAL STANDARD BOOK NUMBER 0-8102-0380-4 (HARD COVER)
LIBRARY OF CONGRESS CATALOG CARD NO. 77-105521

PRINTED IN THE UNITED STATES OF AMERICA

BOOK DESIGNED BY R. KEITH RICHARDSON

For my father, without whose support I would not
have started these investigations

Contents

Foreword

The purpose of this book, at least my interest in it, has been to examine the way language helps actors and directors discover how a play moves on stage. If this aim sounds obvious, I can only plead my own inability to find anyone who has taken the time to consider the subject in print. Actors and directors (particularly actors) do this almost instinctively. The very way they paraphrase Shakespeare's or Marlowe's characters suggests the continuing need to hear the personal, immediate voice of the character they are playing; but they are, after all, actors, not teachers or critics, and they have no need to chart their own methods. Indeed, they may find that such examination inhibits their natural, creative ability to do it. Directors are a little more verbal about their occupations, but, at least to date, they have been generally more concerned with the pictures on stage than with the verbal structures that have suggested those pictures. Or else, like Peter Brook in his recent *The Empty Space* (Atheneum, 1968), they have talked about the total effect of theatre rather than examining any particular playwrights.

My choice of plays is wholly selfish. I have dealt generally with those periods of drama that still seem important to most readers and producers of plays, and my choice of plays has been made from those that I either have produced or am interested in someday producing. That is not to say that they have not been produced. *Oedipus Rex, The Beaux' Stratagem, The Three Sisters,* and *The Birthday Party*—to take only the most obvious—are all produced regularly. My only excuse for dealing with them is to suggest ways of getting at values through the language that are sometimes overlooked—or at least not talked about.

Secondary references in the body of the text, when not footnoted, are listed with some comment in the Bibliographical Essay at the end of the book. I have tried to keep footnotes to a minimum, but I have given act-scene references to plays quoted. For all Shakespeare references, including his sonnet "When to the Sessions of Sweet Silent Thought," I have used Hardin Craig's edition of the complete works (Scott, Foresman, 1951). The poems of Donne, Drayton, and Raleigh can all be found in *Poetry of the English Renaissance, 1509–1660* (J. William Hebel and H. H. Hudson, eds., Appleton-Century-Crofts, 1929; reprinted at least as late as 1946). "Provide, Provide" by Robert Frost, referred to in Chapter III, is in the *Complete Poems of Robert Frost* (Holt, Rinehart and Winston, 1969). The Jebb *Oedipus,* referred to in Chapter II, is most easily available in *Complete Greek Drama* (W. J. Oates and Eugene O'Neill, eds., 2 vols., Random House, 1938). The other translations are identified in the text or in the Bibliographical Essay.

In Chapter IV both *The Way of the World* and *The Beaux' Stratagem* are easy to come by; I have used the paperback editions *William Congreve: Complete Plays* (Alexander Charles Ewald, ed., Hill and Wang, 1956) and *George Farquhar: Four Plays* (edited, with an Introduction and Notes by William Archer, Hill and Wang, 1959). Vanbrugh's *The Relapse* is harder to obtain, but is in *Sir John Vanbrugh* (Introduction and Notes by A. E. H. Swain, A. A. Wyn, Inc., Mermaid Series, 1949). I do hope that this edition will soon be reprinted in paperback. Sheridan's *The School for Scandal* is in a paperback collection, *Richard Brinsley Sheridan: Six Plays* (edited with an Introduction by Louis Kronenberger, Hill and Wang, 1957).

In Chapter V, though I only touch on him, it is worth noting that George Bernard Shaw's plays are available in the edition I used (Odham Press, n.d.); it is almost complete and very inexpensive. As for Marlowe's *Dr. Faustus,* the text of which is always in debate, I have used Leo Kirschbaum's edition, *The Plays of Christopher Marlowe* (Meridian Books, World Publishing Company, 1962). Not only is this edition in paperback form, but Kirschbaum's introduction is very helpful to a producer. Anyone doing the play may want to consult other texts, but this is an excellent beginning. And finally, *The Duchess of Malfi* quotations are from *Webster & Tourneur* (Introduction by J. A. Symonds, Hill and Wang, 1956).

Everyman is another play that exists in many versions. I have used John Gassner's modern version, which appears in his *Treasury of the Theatre* (Vol. I, Simon and Schuster, 1952).

Murder in the Cathedral and *Death of a Salesman* are easily obtainable. I have used T. S. Eliot, *Complete Poems and Plays* (Harcourt, Brace, 1952) for the former, and *Arthur Miller's Collected Plays* (Viking Press, 1957) for the latter. Rochelle Owens' *Futz* is out in a collection of her plays: *Futz and What Came After* (Random House, 1968). And Shepard's *La Turista* can be found in a single-play paperback edition (Bobbs-Merrill, 1968).

I would like to give my thanks to many people, but particularly to those colleagues at the University of California at Riverside who some years ago taught me how to read. To William Arrowsmith and Douglass Parker for introducing me to Greek drama, to Milton Miller for forcing me to understand Shakespeare, and to Thomas Edwards and Marshall Van Deusen for listening.

W. L. S.

Language in Drama

I*

Introduction: Tone of Voice in Drama

The major concern in the following pages—indeed, the unifying center of this book—is the conviction that language, particularly language as used by classic dramatists, has never really been attended to as the prime tool with which a producer works to understand a play not only in general thematic terms but also in very particular character terms. Actors are most certainly aware of the importance of the way an idea is phrased in their search for an honest way to let us see it, to find the correct manner or gesture to support the idea correctly. But then, actors act—they don't write about how they act. The same is true, I suppose, of most directors, and those few who do talk about what they do have not, to my knowledge, talked very specifically about how language is working or how it informs them. There are exceptions, and I would pay with reverence my enormous debt to Granville-Barker, whose *Prefaces to Shakespeare* are not only a continual delight but of inexpressible assistance in my understanding of what goes on in those plays he talks about.

But it was not until 1956, when I read an article by the late Yvor Winters, that I became aware of how really little had been done by producers of drama to define how the tools—the words they dealt with—influenced or delimited what they did. Mr. Winters made some rather startling statements about the drama. He made some rather startling statements about a good number of other things as

---

* This chapter is a revision and expansion of my essay "A Play: Scenario or Poem" in Robert W. Corrigan and James L. Rosenberg, eds., *The Art of the Theatre* (San Francisco: Chandler Publishing Company, 1964). The essay originally appeared in the *Tulane Drama Review*, V:2, December 1960.

well, but his remarks about the dramatic form in general and *Macbeth* in particular ask, I think, for some kind of comment.[1] Winters was a good critic; the issues he raised are important issues, issues that should be considered by anyone seriously interested in the dramatic form. And though I think he was wrong, he was wrong in an important way.

The position that Winters took in regard to this subject is most clearly stated in the following paragraph:

Let us suppose that the dramatist is imitating the speech of a character of moderate intelligence in a situation of which the character does not in any serious sense understand the meaning. This presents an almost insoluble problem. If a poet is endeavoring to communicate his own best understanding of a situation, that is one thing. If he is endeavoring to communicate approximately a plausible misunderstanding of a situation on the part of an imaginary character much less intelligent than himself, that is quite another. He can only guess at the correct measure of stupidity which may be proper to such a character in a given situation, whether the character is offered as an imitation or as a plausible imitation of an imitation; and whether he is successful or not, he will still be writing poetry which as poetry will be of an inferior kind. Exactly what is the target? It seems to me that the whole business must in the nature of the case be a rough approximation—and rough approximations are unfortunate affairs in the fine arts.

This insistence on "rough approximations" in drama seems to me, quite simply, not true. On the contrary, if the dramatist is good, he is attempting by "his own best understanding of a [human] situation" to communicate through that complex of attitudes of all of the characters in a play not only what the characters think but what the playwright thinks; and he does this, as does any literary artist, first and foremost with words. Words, to be sure, which are to be spoken by an actor on a stage with all the machinery the stage offers, but words put together in such a fashion that they tell the actor how they are to be spoken and what gestures and mannerisms should accompany them. The words, then, should guide the actor. If he is a good actor, he allows them to, and the result is a combination of word and gesture that creates the attitude to which we are to respond.

[1] The article, "Problems for the Modern Critic of Literature," appeared in the *Hudson Review* (Autumn 1956). Of special interest is Section VII, pp. 363–371.

CHAPTER I

Since this attitude is originally created and judged by the playwright through the manner in which he puts together the words which create that attitude, that character, he is not imitating "an imaginary character much less intelligent than himself," any more than a lyric poet is imitating a lover much more emotionally involved than himself when he writes a love lyric. I don't know what kind of imitation is going on in the first line of Donne's "The Canonization," but I do feel as I read through the poem that it is an attitude carefully controlled and qualified not by the lover but by the poet.

I suspect that what I would call Winters' confusion in regard to drama resulted in part from his concept of character. In the course of the article, he spent some time looking at Macbeth's soliloquy "Is this a dagger which I see before me." His most extended objections I hope to deal with later, but I would like to look at one comment here. In referring to one part of the soliloquy, Winters wrote:

It seems unlikely that Macbeth in real life would have spoken anything so elaborate, but had he done so it would doubtless have been violent; and it would certainly have been composed of stereotypes, because at this stage of his development he had only a stereotyped understanding of what he was doing.

Now such a view is understandable only if one believes that a playwright is communicating "a plausible misunderstanding of a situation on the part of an imaginary character much less intelligent than himself." If, however, one conceives of a character as a carefully defined series of believably connected attitudes toward a series of events—attitudes, furthermore, that came out of the real head of Shakespeare rather than the fictional head of Macbeth— there is the possibility, at least, of a very different evaluation of drama and of *Macbeth* than that given by Winters. The problem is how one is to know which head is talking.

The way to discover the poet's view in a play, at least in a play of Shakespeare, is, it seems to me, very similar to the way one discovers a poet's view in a lyric poem. To be sure, the tools in the two genres are not identical. A lyric poet uses language exclusively. A good playwright uses contrasting scenes, contrasting characters, even contrasting actions as well. But he creates his scenes, his actions, and his characters with language. If he is good, with very precise language.

One understands a character in a play (and I assume it is clear that by "character" I mean that complex of attitudes that define one point of view in a play, a point of view called Macbeth, Lady Macbeth, and so on) by examining all of the speeches that create it. And "all," here, means not only all of the speeches of that particular character, but all of those speeches given by other characters that refer to it. All of these speeches create the context in which any single speech must be examined, just as the fourteen lines of a sonnet create the context in which any single line is understood.

As a consequence, when Winters evaluated the "Is this a dagger which I see before me" soliloquy as "not very good poetry," as "an imitation of a second-rate intelligence in a distraught condition," without apparently any sense of the mind of Shakespeare, he was, it seems to me, evaluating badly, if for no other reason than that he was not looking at the whole context of the "poem." To judge a single speech in a play in the same way as one judges a single sonnet is unfair, not because speeches in poetic drama can't be examined on the same terms as a lyric, but because, unless the whole context in which that single speech operates is considered (namely, the whole dramatic sequence of events and speeches that has preceded it) , one is not examining that speech on the same terms on which he examines a sonnet. It is more like examining the couplet without reference to the preceding twelve lines.

By the use of scene juxtaposition, previous speeches by a given character, and speeches by other characters both to and about the given one, a dramatist is able to create a point of view, a character, which not only is a part of the experience at which the playwright is looking but is also, in the *way* he is presented, put in some kind of evaluating relation to that experience. This is not to say that any single character or point of view in the play is the same as the playwright's; obviously, it cannot be more than one part of the total attitude expressed in the play. But I do wish to make clear my belief that we should be able to hear what is wrong with Macbeth, whether Macbeth knows it or not, by the way in which he is made to talk. In doing this, Shakespeare need no more "guess at the correct measure of stupidity which may be proper to such a character in a given situation," as Winters would have us believe, than the poet need guess at the particular attitude he takes in any given poem. Macbeth's attitude came out of Shakespeare's head, too. In other words, in a good play the dramatist evaluates the experience he examines through the way all of the characters in the play speak about and react to the particular experience (whether it be love or murder) that the playwright is examining, just as surely as the poet evaluates the experience he is looking at in, let us say, a good sonnet. In both cases the language operates in such a way as to let us know the playwright's and the lyric poet's attitude toward the experience being examined.

Lest all this seem rather vague talk, let me look for a moment at two short poems, poems which operate in the way I have been suggesting the drama operates. They are poems which evaluate an experience by creating an attitude toward that experience which looks, on the surface, to be that of "an imaginary character," a speaker at any rate, of less intelligence than the poet. Obviously the attitude I am looking at here is the whole attitude, because the poem is the whole work. To make a direct parallel to a play, one would have to examine the whole play, all of the attitudes expressed in it. The method used in both cases, however, is similar.

The first of these speaker-poets I want to consider is Sir Walter Raleigh in his poem "The Lie." As one reads through this poem, he may feel, as I do, that the tone of voice of the poet (if he hears a tone of voice) is a little too angry, a little too excited in his condemnations, even a little naïve. The series of commands culminating in the next-to-last verse,

> Tell faith it's fled the city;
> Tell how the country erreth;
> Tell, manhood shakes off pity,
> Tell, virtue least preferred:

though saved from preachiness by both the rhythm and the rhyme, sounds nevertheless a little overstated—and I think, consciously so. It is, I think, just this sense of overstatement that allows for the power of "blabbing" in the last verse.

> So when thou hast, as I
> Commanded thee, done blabbing,
> Because to give the lie
> Deserves no less than stabbing,
>   Stab at thee he that will—
>   No stab the soul can kill.

One has heard the overinsistence, the overannoyance of the speaker at the viciousness of the world around him in these earlier commands, and one is a little suspicious of such zeal, a zeal that almost suggests naïveté, until the sudden appearance of "blabbing" makes clear the knowledge and the sophistication of the speaker. We see clearly what the carefully controlled rhythm has suggested, that the speaker realizes the kind of overstatement he is making, that he realizes, even though everything he says is true, that one doesn't in some active way *do* anything about it. And the sophistication of the speaker, made evident through the way he says what he says, is what finally determines our own reaction to the poem, our own sense of Raleigh's maturity.

I think much the same process goes on in many lyrics, even in such formal structures as sonnets. I mean here not only those sonnets with a directly implied second person like Drayton's "Since There's No Help, Come Let Us Kiss and Part," but any sonnet, Shakespeare's "When to the Sessions of Sweet Silent Thought," for example. I have heard the latter praised for its beautiful alliteration or for its legal imagery. At the same time I have heard it damned for its weak couplet. It seems to me that both kinds of comments are legitimate, but I can only really put them all together as part of a single reading, by referring to the speaker in the poem. One remembers the abundance of *s*'s in the first line, and the *w*'s in the fourth, and occasionally, particularly in that first line, one falls prey to its sweetness, overlooking the fact that, as the poem moves on, it really gets pretty sloppy and sentimental, not obviously, but surely. There is something a little too self-conscious in drowning an eye "unused to flow," in the repetition of "grieve" in "grieve at grievances," in those "precious friends" hid in "death's dateless night," and certainly in the precious blubbering of "fore-bemoaned moan." This is a grief that one hesitates to take too seriously. The speaker's lace handkerchief almost shows. Even the legal imagery is a little untender, a little conscious. And it seems to me that it is precisely *because* this is so self-conscious that the couplet (weak as it is to turn the poet from heartfelt grief) is about right *here*. For a really felt grief this thinking-on-thee-dear-friend to end all sorrows is a little easy. If this is all it takes to remove the pain, it couldn't have been much. Yet if we hear those first twelve lines as a nostalgic sigh of pleasureful self-pity, a delight in easy tears, then the change back to normalcy with the ease the couplet suggests seems about right; it seems to evaluate the kind of grief here delineated for what it is worth. And one feels the poet, or the speaker here, appreciates this feeling for what it is worth in a way that Shelley, for example, doesn't usually manage.

I mention these poems only to suggest that one of the ways we are able to evaluate and judge the experience the poet presents to us, is by hearing the speaker, by hearing in the poet's tone of voice his particular pose as his choice of words and rhythms define it for us. It may be true that the structural principle in the short poem is logic, as Winters insisted, but we do sometimes get what he called the "total understanding," "not merely the rational but the emotional as well," by evaluating the speaker and his logic in the poem, by evaluating the particular attitude that the poet adopts in the particular poem under examination. And just as we may hear the poet in a poem *through the speaker the poet creates for us* in that poem, so we hear the dramatist through the characters the dramatist creates for us. To be sure, we hear many more speakers in the drama, and we are usually presented with a greater number of experiences, though not unrelated ones. As a consequence, the totality of the play may be a good deal more difficult to define than the totality of a single lyric, but not, I think, because of an inherent "weakness" in the form.

If, for example, I were to look at that soliloquy of Macbeth's that Winters dismissed so easily as "not very good poetry" in its total context, something Winters did not do, I think it might even be found to be fairly good, not simply the imitation of a "distraught condition" which gives "the actor opportunity to ham it," but a surprisingly precise delineation of both Macbeth's condition at this point in the play and Shakespeare's judgment of that condition. Despite its familiarity, I wish to quote it in full so that I can make specific reference:

> Is this a dagger which I see before me,
> The handle toward my hand? Come, let me clutch thee.
> I have thee not, and yet I see thee still.
> Art thou not, fatal vision, sensible
> To feeling as to sight: or art thou but   5
> A dagger of the mind, a false creation,
> Proceeding from the heat-oppressèd brain?

I see thee yet, in form as palpable
As this which now I draw.
Thou marshall'st me the way that I was going;   10
And such an instrument I was to use.
Mine eyes are made the fools o'the other senses,
Or else worth all the rest; I see thee still,
And on thy blade and dudgeon gouts of blood,
Which was not so before. There's no such thing: 15
It is the bloody business which informs
Thus to mine eyes. Now o'er the one half-world
Nature seems dead, and wicked dreams abuse
The curtain'd sleep; witchcraft celebrates
Pale Hecate's offerings, and wither'd murder,   20
Alarum'd by his sentinel, the wolf,
Whose howl's his watch, thus with his stealthy pace,
With Tarquin's ravishing strides, towards his design
Moves like a ghost. Thou sure and firm-set earth,
Hear not my steps, which way they walk, for fear   25
Thy very stones prate of my whereabout,
And take the present horror from the time,
Which now suits with it. Whiles I threat, he lives:
Words to the heat of deeds too cold breath gives.
I go, and it is done; the bell invites me.   30
Hear it not, Duncan; for it is a knell
That summons thee to heaven or to hell.   [II, 1]

Winters seemed fairly happy with the first seven lines but found the
next ten redundant and the following eight (beginning "Now" in
line 17 and ending "ghost" in line 24) inappropriate to the character speaking them. The last eight lines he conveniently ignored.
The repetitions that bothered Winters are obvious enough—the
similar phrases in the third, eighth, and thirteenth lines, and the
material following each. In the third line it appears in the last half
of that line, "and yet I see thee still"; in the eighth it opens the
line, "I see thee yet"; and in the thirteenth it ends the line, in the
form "I see thee still." This insistence on seeing, on not being able
not to see, seemed redundant to Winters. He would have been
happier, apparently, if the soliloquy moved from the end of the
seventh line to the middle of the fifteenth. This is what the lyric
poet who "is endeavoring to communicate his own best understanding of a [human] situation" would have done. Now, it's my
own belief that if he had done this, he would not have made the

same, nor as clear, a judgment of the particular condition being examined, as Shakespeare does by that repetition.

The emphasis in this soliloquy, particularly in the first fourteen and one-half lines, is on sight, and this emphasis is not there so that some actor can "ham it" but in order to say something about the importance Macbeth places on what he can see, on what he can determine with his five immediate senses. If he can *see* that dagger here, it must be real, and not a dagger of the mind. If he can convince himself that "There's no such thing," for he would like to persuade himself that *things,* like daggers, have tangible reality or none at all, then he can dismiss this vision as a "wicked dream." One of the major struggles for Macbeth throughout the play is to persuade himself that the immediate, the tangible, is worth more than the imagined, that a kingdom on earth will compensate for a possible damnation in hell, that some kind of immediate and tangible protection (no man of woman born, Birnam Wood's moving) can keep him from a distant and perhaps only imagined hellfire. Hell can't be seen except through an imagination, prompted perhaps by a conscience, but it is not physically demonstrable. Hell manifests itself in images, in "wicked dreams," and though in the course of the play one is persuaded, as is Macbeth, that those tangible, literal, immediate antidotes to his imagination will not remain on a tangible, immediate level, here that answer is still in doubt.

Macbeth would deny his imagination, his conscience, if he could, though he knows the difficulty. He said, in the previous scene:

> If the assassination
> Could trammel up the consequence, and catch
> With his surcease success; that but this blow
> Might be the be-all and the end-all here,
> But here, upon this bank and shoal of time
> We'ld jump the life to come. But in these cases
> We still have judgment here;   [I, 7]

The power of that conscience and its instrument, imagined image, has been thoroughly examined by Macbeth, so thoroughly that at the end of the soliloquy he is ready to admit the impossibility of denying it. He doesn't attempt to deny it, until Lady Macbeth's beautiful chop logic lulls his judgment:

                              then you were a man;
        And to be more than what you were, you would
        Be so much more the man. [I, 7]

Logic is not Macbeth's strong point. His judgment operates most
surely through his imagination, subrationally rather than rationally. When Lady Macbeth appeals in this pseudo-rational fashion,
Macbeth is swayed—swayed not by the rationality but by the most
universal of female tricks, "You don't love me," "You're afraid,"
and the like. Such arguments convince because the woman who uses
them is an immediate, tangible, desirable presence that cuts off
imagination, Macbeth's surest judge.

    The preceding scene (the one that has included both the "If the
assassination" soliloquy quoted above and the scene with Lady
Macbeth) is as necessary in considering both the meaning and
judgment implicit in this speech as is the first line or two of a
sonnet. The preceding scene in part accounts for the appearance of
the dagger at this point in the play. If Lady Macbeth's presence
could stifle the imagination, her absence gives free reign for it to
operate again—and operate it does, to counsel Macbeth against
murder. But now Macbeth would fight it, would fight it with his
commitment to the present, to the immediate, the tangible. If he
can convince himself that this dagger is simply a vision of the mind
and not something real, a figment not a fact, then he can reject it;
but as long as he can *see* it, as he sees his own very real dagger, that
long he can't deny it, that long it is tangible, touchable evidence to
be trusted, attended to. Only when he sees those "gouts of blood"
that Winters so disliked, can he reject it as imaginative, as something irrational, something not to be attended to—a "wicked
dream." It is this last detail that makes it not a real dagger, but a
dagger of the mind, that convinces him that his eyes are made "the
fools o'the other senses." And the irony of this line is not accidental.
Macbeth may judge his eyes as fools because they see what isn't
there, but the audience knows they see through Macbeth's imagination what is very much there—a conscience that knows such action
as murder cannot be evaluated in the pragmatic terms that Macbeth would like to use.

    Obviously, then, I do not think the lines redundant. The "I see
thee" impresses the importance of this aspect of Macbeth's method
of evaluating. The deletion of the repetition would give us a much

more rationally adequate Macbeth indeed. Nor is the image of the dagger "abandoned" as Winters insisted, any more than the theme of midnight horror is "taken up"—as if the poet were tired of the first and looked around haphazardly for the second. Macbeth has fought his vision of the dagger in order to get rid of it, and apparently he has succeeded. It was but one of those "wicked dreams" which "abuse the curtain'd sleep." The tone changes and Macbeth again appears confident; yet he gives himself away, or rather Shakespeare gives him away. These wicked dreams which Macbeth would dismiss remind him of "witchcraft," "Pale Hecate's offerings," and although he may not note the close juxtaposition of those wicked dreams to warning daggers on the one side and the witches in the play on the other, the audience does, Shakespeare did. Nor is it accidental that those "wicked dreams" which counseled wisely, when ignored, lead on to murder in general, to Tarquin (who also ravished innocence), to Macbeth himself: "Thou sure and firm-set earth, / Hear not my steps."

This seems to me good dramatic writing, a speech in which both our understanding of Macbeth and our understanding of Shakespeare's judgment of Macbeth are made quite nicely clear. I understand Winters' belief, already mentioned, that this last passage is weak because Macbeth would not have spoken them "in real life." But such a position is only possible if one insists on judging dramatic fictions as real persons. Macbeth is not a *real* person. We know no more what he would do "in real life" than we know what the speaker in Shakespeare's sonnet might do "in real life." The series of connected attitudes that we call character in a play come finally out of the playwright's mouth, not that of some real-life character whose perceptions are "somewhat sharpened" and whose thoughts are "somewhat accelerated and heightened by the situation." A good playwright doesn't start with real people in a play; he starts with attitudes. One sees these attitudes defined and qualified in the context of an ordered fiction. As one watches or reads a play and hears that point of view called a character, he does not constantly—if ever, I think—refer it to some concept of a real Macbeth with a life outside the play.

The difference between this speech and the "standard huffing speech" that Winters would have liked to make of it is precisely Shakespeare's ability to show, through a careful choice both of words and of verbal connections, the creation of a conceivable and believable psychological attitude. No simple "huffing speech" ever managed this. The language Macbeth uses in that "Now o'er the one half-world" section gives away the very rationalization that he thinks will protect him. If the dagger is a bad dream, so are the witches that lead to murder. So, too, the wolf and Tarquin, though they may have incidental meaning to Macbeth, do not to us. If, finally, Macbeth can dismiss the *words* with which he has examined his plight ("Whiles I threat, he lives") as talk, the audience, even the reader, cannot. Those words have given Macbeth away, in a way he may not at this point realize; the audience, however, has no such difficulty.

All of this annoyance with Winters' easy dismissal of poetic drama, or for that matter all drama, is not simply aimed at this one critic. It comes, in part at least, from the fact that Winters could and did come off so absolutely unchallenged. His opinion of actors in particular and drama in general was not new, though it was stated more clearly in the article under discussion than anywhere else I know; yet no one interested in drama bothers to attend to him. Perhaps this is because his opinion is thought too wrong-headed to merit attention. Perhaps, however, it is because those interested in drama are uncomfortable on his chosen ground, the word. This latter discomfort seems to me unfortunate, even dangerous, for a serious dramatic analyst or critic. It suggests that what to me is the most important part of the play, the language, is getting very short shrift. One wonders if there is agreement with Winters' final conclusion about drama:

The play in prose—let us say by Etherege, or Congreve, or Shaw—would seem to offer fewer obstacles as regards performance, for the text is close to normal speech and demands less of the performers. But such a play offers less to the reader, for it enjoys the advantages neither of poetic style on the one hand, nor of the prose analysis of the novel on the other; it comes close to being a mere scenario, dependent for its success upon the mechanical aids of the theatre.

I would hope not. It seems to me that good drama, whether in poetry or prose, defines experience by expressing attitudes toward it just as good lyrics do. Obviously the drama does not do it in precisely the same way lyrics do. It has, certainly, the actors and the scenery to which Winters refers. But most good drama also has words, words used with a good deal of precision, enough precision to direct the actor, the setting, and those other "mechanical aids of the theatre." The words in a play, not only by Shakespeare, but by Congreve or Shaw as well, operate precisely and definitively to create those attitudes we call character. In many plays—I think particularly of the rhyme in Molière's *The Misanthrope,* though it is also true in the careful prose of Congreve—these words define the whole society in which such attitudes exist.

In Congreve, for example, I can hardly see, even in his least successful plays, that the language is particularly "close to normal speech," "demands less of the performers," or is in any way "close to being a mere scenario." In *The Double Dealer,* one of the funniest and sharpest portraits is that of Lady Pliant, a lady who has a very positive, though altogether unclear, notion of right and wrong. And it is through her speech that this is made clear. Listen to her talk to a would-be seducer: ". . . . you are very alluring—And say so many fine Things, and nothing is so moving to me as a fine Thing." This is not sloppy writing on Congreve's part, but carefully controlled vagueness that allows us to see what kind of woman she is, at the same time that it makes clear Congreve's judgment of her. The same is true in the apparently careless rhythm and abundant alliteration in her acceptance of that would-be seducer:

O, you have conquer'd, sweet, melting, moving sir, you have conquer'd! What heart of marble can refrain to weep, and yield to such sad sayings!

Oh, I yield myself all up to your uncontrollable embraces!—Say, thou dear, dying man, when, where, and how? [IV, 1]

Again this is no more careless writing than Shakespeare's "forebemoaned moan." We know this woman, as we know the speaker in that poem, by the way she talks, not so much by what she says as by how she says it. And in both cases, it seems to me, the writer's judgment is made evident through the way he lets his characters speak.

This is typical in Congreve. Not only in *Love for Love* and *The Way of the World,* where one might expect it, but in such an early and relatively little appreciated work as *The Old Bachelor.* Listen to Sir Joseph Wittol, a naïve country lord, thank Sharper for, as he thinks, saving his life. In point of fact, Sharper has done no such thing. He has been, and still is, fleecing him of half his income:

. . . your goodness, which like an inundation will, I hope, totally immerge the recollection of my error, and leave me floating in your sight upon the full blown bladders of repentence by the help of which I shall once more hope to swim into your favour. [II, 1]

The stupid fish swimming blandly, if blindly, into the net is Wittol's position entirely. The excited overenthusiasm in "bladders of repentence" and "inundation" are part of the flabby insecurity of Sir Joseph. And it is the words and their phrasing that convince us. Character is depicted for the actor, and for the reader, by the *way* he speaks.

The same is true of Shaw. In *Candida,* for example, we could hardly accept the truth of Marchbanks' evaluation of Morell as having "the gift of gab, nothing more and nothing less," of feeding his wife on "sermons, stale perorations, mere rhetoric" unless we had heard some of this ourselves. Listen to one such peroration spoken by Morell to Marchbanks shortly before the above-mentioned outburst:

You will be one of the makers of the Kingdom of Heaven on earth; and —who knows?—you may be a master builder where I am only a humble journeyman; for don't think, my boy, that I cannot see in you, young as you are, promise of higher powers than I can ever pretend to. I well know that it is in the poet that the holy spirit of man—the god within him—is most godlike. It should make you tremble to think of that—to think that the heavy burthen and great gift of a poet may be laid upon you. [Act I]

It is not accidental or careless writing that allows us to hear the public speaker in this speech. The rhetorical building of suspense in the "who knows?" which interrupts the first sentence, or the similar interruption by "the god within him" in the second, and the beautifully forced "bur*th*en" in the last are all carefully controlled verbal patterns to define a certain kind of attitude. Rephrase Morell, let him speak in a truly sincere fashion, and you destroy him.

But why belabor the obvious? Winters undoubtedly knew better than his generalization suggests. I sometimes think he generalized in order to annoy, to create opposition. The only pity here is that in dramatic analysis at least, he doesn't create more. A careful ear in drama, attention to phrasing, has seldom been given less attention than it seems to get today. The popularity of Eugene O'Neill, who can't write at all, the verbal pretension of Christopher Fry, and the near destruction of language altogether in the work of Ionesco attest to the insensitive ear not only of the playwright and his audience, but of the dramatic critic as well. So-called method actors grunt well because most modern drama doesn't ask them to do anything else. But such inattention on the part of playwrights, actors, audience, and critic alike does not mean that the dramatic form is weak. It means only that full advantage is not being taken of it.

Winters, I can't help feeling, was very wrong, but until attention, real attention, is paid to the area in which he condemned drama, his opinion will have more unarguable weight than it deserves, and many plays will be less good in production than they ought to be.

My hope in the following chapters is not to attend simply to a defense of drama as a form or even to a definition of it. I am already committed to the form, and definitions only confuse me. I do, however, hope to suggest to actors and directors, to anyone who is interested in the problems of acting and directing, the importance of the ways in which words are put together and how that patterning structures the event that the actor or director wishes to make clear to an audience. To be sure, drama is action, but unless that action is carried out totally in pantomime, one of the main means of telling us what that action is and how the characters in a play respond to it is the language. It is of how exactly producers of a text can make use of language that I want to speak in this book.

Choruses in Greek Tragedy

If one is committed to drama, there is no way to avoid Greek tragedy—nor, I hope, any desire to. But the very way in which Greek drama works asks for some careful examination of at least one term that is vital to a discussion of language, indeed of drama, and that is very different in *Oedipus,* for example, than in *Lear.* The term is "character." When one gets to Shakespeare, and indeed from then on in drama, one can in some way talk very concretely about character. In fact, one must; I hope I will be able to suggest how, when I get to Shakespeare. But when one moves back in time, to Sophocles and Euripides (even more so in Aeschylus), one is moving away from character, at least from character in its most definable sense, however seldom our discussions admit it: character as particular personality.

While it is true that Greek drama, like any drama, needs, in its episodes, its single speeches, an actor's attention to what underlies that speech, the emotional and psychological underpinnings are much more general. How can I explain that statement, except to say that Oedipus really is Everyman in a more immediate way than Lear is. One hopes as he hears Oedipus that, put in the same situation, discovering the same or a similar kind of horror at the way fate operates, he would have the strength to face the discovery in the same way Oedipus does. While this can be said of Lear, I think one is much more immediately aware of a cranky old man, already a portrait somewhat removed from our sense of our best self. The sense of character in a Greek tragedy has somewhat the same relation to Shakespeare's sense of character as the frieze on the Parthe-

non has to the *Laocoön*. In the former we have none of the
particularity of a human being in a specific situation showing us a
very particular response. If Athena directs Hercules in his labors,
both the goddess and the human do their task. There is no sense of
triumph in Athena or of pain in Hercules. There is a strange,
idealized sense of what is to be done and the best response man can
give to doing it. In the *Laocoön* a very particular man responds
with very particular pain to the serpents that entwine him; we are
asked to respond to that pain. Or take one other example. If one
looks at the sixth-century B.C. statue of *Zeus at Artemidorus* and
compares it to the *Apollo Belvedere,* one is again aware of a particularity in regard to the human shape. The *Zeus* (perhaps a
Poseidon) stands in a generalized position, with little or no expression on his face and with his arm raised to throw his thunderbolt (or
brandish his trident). Again there is no particular expression
immediately suggested by what he is doing—no joy, no triumph,
only acceptance. The *Apollo,* on the contrary, sitting on his hip, has
a strangely effeminate quality, and the almost indolent smile on his
face tells us something very specific about his view of the world. He
has postures, he has attitudes, he has a particular point of view that
is different from that of other Apollos. In the same way Oedipus is
all men, Lear is a very particular man. In both cases we make
generalizations to our own experience, but the distance one travels
in Shakespeare is from a much greater particularity than in
Sophocles.

That is not to say that language is not important in Greek
drama; it is to say that tone of voice must be looked at in a much
larger sense. We are usually working with a much larger event in
Greek tragedy, and it is important that we hear speeches which echo
that size, which, indeed, are not too particular. Too often in
modern translations we hear of the need for a verbal structure that
an actor can speak, the consequence of which may be a prosified,
simplified view of the speaker. Perhaps this is most true in choruses,
since they are at once the hardest elements to make clear and the
most moving when they are so.

I am not a Greek scholar, so my preferences in translation may
not really suggest the original, but I think some quotations can
suggest the differences which I see. Let me quote two translations of
the first ode from *Oedipus*. Both, it seems to me, are clear, but they

are immensely different in feeling and in what they suggest should be projected. The first is from Cavander's translation, of which Robert Corrigan says in "A Note on the Translation":[1]

It is eminently actable, and the language of the choral passages opens up in such a way that we can sense the Theban Elders moving and chanting in a manner befitting the ritualistic conventions of the Greek theater.

I quote only the first strophe and antistrophe, but it gives, I think, a fair sense of the emotion underlying the appeal to God and the size of the fear that motivates the speakers:

From golden Delphi Apollo replies to Thebes
And the words of heaven send a warning.
As a lyre is strung and tightened, so we
Are tightened by fear.
As a lyre trembles, so we tremble at the touch of fear.
Apollo, god of healing, god of newness,
We fear you, and the commands you send to humble us.
Do you ask a new submission? Or is your command
The same as we hear in every wind, and every season, and every year?
Only the child of golden hope, whose voice   1
Will never die, only the spirit of truth can tell us.
First in my prayers is the goddess Athene, the daughter of Zeus;
Second, her sister Artemis, who is queen in Thebes,
For she sits at our country's heart, pure and honoured,
In a temple like the sun. And third in our prayer   1
Is Phoebus Apollo, whose arm reaches over all the world.
Come three times to drive our wrongs before you!
If ever in the past, when evil and blindness
Rose like a wave, when grief was burning in our city,
If ever you banished that grief,
Come now to help us.   2

There is no numbering our sorrows;
The whole country is sick, and mortal will and human mind
Are no weapons to defend us.
The great earth whom we call our mother   2
Is barren and dead; women weep in the pain of childbirth
But they fall sick and die.
Look, can you see the dying go following each other,
Gliding like gentle birds, quicker
Then the restless flash of fire that will never sleep,   3
The dying on their flight to the shore

[1] Sophocles, *Oedipus the King* (Kenneth Cavander, trans., Chandler Publishing Company, 1961).

18   CHAPTER II

Where evening sits like a goddess?
The city of the dying goes countless away
And the children of life fall to the earth,
The toys of death,   35
With no pity and no remembering tears.

In the rest of our city wives and mothers
Stand grey at the altars,
Which tell us of a certainty resisting the seas of doubt;
They weep, pray, plead for release   40
From the harsh revenge which heaven brings.
A cry for healing rises and burns above the still crowd
That mourns in the city.
Send us strength that will look kindly on us,
Golden daughter of Zeus.   45
Ares, the god of war, confronts us, bitter in his cruelty,
And his shout burns like fire;
But his war is fought with no armour, and Ares
Carries no shield, for he brings his conflict
Into the moment of our birth and death.   50
Oh turn him flying down the winds, turn him
Back and dash him from our country
Into the wide chambers where Amphitrite sleeps,
Or to the lonely cliffs of Thrace where the seas
Allow no guests. For Ares comes to finish   55
The deadly work left undone by the night.
Zeus, you are the lord of lightning, lord of fire,
Destroy him with your thunder, crush our enemy!

Lord Apollo, god in the sun, we pray for your light;
Strike with your golden spears and your hands of fire,   60
Strike to protect us.
We pray for Artemis to bring her chaste fires,
Which we see her carry like a shining torch across
The mountains where the wolf runs.
I call you, the god with the golden crown,   65
Born in our country, Bacchus,
With the fire of wine in your cheek,
And the voice of wine in your shout,
Come with your pine branch burning, and your Maenads
Following the light, the fire of heaven's madness   70
In their eyes, come to guard us against the treacherous power
Who goes to war with justice and the harmony of heaven!

This ode from the stricken Thebans follows Creon's return from
Delphi with the news of the defilement in Thebes and the need to

drive it out. It is clearly a prayer to Apollo for relief, for more than relief, for understanding. The fear that tightens them comes from their inability to understand God's word, though certainly they can and do respond to it with terror. What does God want? "Only," they say with apparent conviction, "the child of golden hope, whose voice / Will never die, only the spirit of truth can tell us." And so they pray, in a rather formulary manner, almost mechanically, "First in my prayers is the goddess Athene, . . . Second, her sister Artemis, who is queen . . . And third in our prayer / Is Phoebus Apollo, whose arm reaches over all the world." Then, almost like an incantation, "Come three times to drive our wrongs before you."

Certainly there is nothing difficult to speak here. It is good, clear, straightforward English. It suggests, however, a populace that is in no doubt of its final survival. In an almost ritualistic manner, but with apparent conviction in its efficacy, the chorus makes its plea to divinity. There is nothing surrounding the incantation to suggest other than the suppliants' hope. They are in no way unsure of their salvation, or perhaps more accurately they are not so distraught but what they can express their grief in a rational, controlled way. Listen to the second three lines, the enlargement of their fear:

> As a lyre is strung and tightened, so we
> Are tightened by fear.
> As a lyre trembles, so we tremble at the touch of fear.

Fearful to be sure, but it is a fear that can be expressed, that can be incorporated in a controlled simile. For comparison's sake, let me quote another translation. This is the Fitts version:[2]

> What is God singing in his profound   STROPHE 1
> Delphi of gold and shadow?
> What oracle for Thebes, the sunwhipped city?
>
> Fear unjoints me, the roots of my heart tremble.
>
> Now I remember, O Healer, your power, and wonder:
> Will you send doom like a sudden cloud, or weave it
> Like nightfall of the past?
> Speak, speak to us, issue of holy sound:
> Dearest to our expectancy: be tender!

[2] *The Oedipus Cycle* (Dudley Fitts and Robert Fitzgerald, trans., Harvest Book, Harcourt, Brace, 1939) .

Let me pray to Athenê, the immortal daughter of Zeus, ANTISTROPHE 1
And to Artemis her sister
Who keeps her famous throne in the market ring,
And to Apollo, bowman at the far butts of heaven—

O gods, descend! Like three streams leap against
The fires of our grief, the fires of darkness;
Be swift to bring us rest!

As in the old time from the brilliant house
Of air you stepped to save us, come again!

Now our afflictions have no end, STROPHE 2
Now all our stricken host lies down
And no man fights off death with his mind;

The noble plowland bears no grain,
And groaning mothers can not bear—

See, how our lives like birds take wing,
Like sparks that fly when a fire soars,
To the shore of the god of evening.

The plague burns on, it is pitiless, ANTISTROPHE 2
Though pallid children laden with death
Lie unwept in the stony ways,

And old gray women by every path
Flock to the strand about the altars

There to strike their breasts and cry
Worship of Phoibos in wailing prayers:
Be kind, God's golden child!

There are no swords in this attack by fire, STROPHE 3
No shields, but we are ringed with cries.
Send the besieger plunging from our homes
Into the vast sea-room of the Atlantic
Or into the waves that foam eastward of Thrace—

For the day ravages what the night spares—

Destroy our enemy, lord of the thunder!
Let him be riven by lightning from heaven!

Phoibos Apollo, stretch the sun's bowstring, ANTISTROPHE 3
That golden cord, until it sing for us,

Flashing arrows in heaven!
                            Artemis, Huntress,
Race with flaring lights upon our mountains!
O scarlet god, O golden-banded brow,
O Theban Bacchos in a storm of Maenads,

Whirl upon Death, that all the Undying hate!
Come with blinding torches, come in joy!

How different the Fitts opening from the Cavander:

What is God singing in his profound
Delphi of gold and shadow?
What oracle for Thebes, the sunwhipped city?

The question has much less sense of an explicable divinity working in a humanly explicable way. Here one cannot even be sure God has sent anything as understandable as a warning. All we hear is the simple question "What is God singing in his profound Delphi . . . ?" And rather than the carefully balanced simile to express the fear, the single line "Fear unjoints me, the roots of my heart tremble." There is also a very real difference in the tone of the prayer. Where Cavander is formulary, Fitts is much more desperate. It is not a prayer of what the chorus will do, but a plea to be heard. And finally, rather than Cavander's almost incantatory "Come three times," there is the real cry for help, "O gods, descend! Like three streams leap against / The fires of our grief."

In the Fitts, one is continually made aware that the prayer is primarily to Apollo, the source of the oracle from Delphi. To be sure, Athene, Athens' own, and Artemis, her sister, and Bacchus all are called, but it is Artemis with her "flaring lights" and Bacchus with his "blinding torches" that are called for. Apollo, the god of light, is at the center of this prayer from his Delphi of "gold and shadow"—Apollo, who speaks to this "sunwhipped city." The imagery continually comes back to this paradox of light that is dark or destructive. Doom is "like a sudden cloud," the three gods are asked to leap like streams against the "fires of darkness," the very lives of the chorus are but "sparks that fly when a fire soars." And it is Zeus and his lightning that are called for to destroy this "attack by fire." And finally, rather than letting the sun whip the city, the final antistrophe begins:

> Phoibos Apollo, stretch the sun's bowstring,
> That golden cord, until it sing for us,
> Flashing arrows in heaven!

All of these images of light and darkness, of sun and shadow, keep not only Apollo before us, but perhaps more importantly the sense of a force that is primal. It is nature itself that is in upheaval here, so that men question their very desire to live and "no man fights off death with his mind."

The sense of formal prayer in the Cavander makes the whole choric plea less basic, less primal in its need, more ordered. One cannot escape the feeling that this chorus sees its plight as the result of some kind of sin. The wives and mothers standing "grey at the altars . . . plead for release / From the harsh revenge which heaven brings." This is very different—much more Christian in its sense of sin and punishment—from the Fitts "old gray women" who cry, "Worship of Phoibus in wailing prayers: / Be kind, God's golden child." There is no assurance of some moral order that man has upset here, only a cry for pity, for kindness. Artemis, for Cavander, comes with "chaste fires," not racing with "flaring lights," and Bacchus is asked to "guard us against the treacherous power / Who goes to war with justice and the harmony of heaven," rather than simply to "Whirl upon Death, that all the Undying hate," to "Come with blinding torches, come in joy!"

I suspect my own preference for the Fitts is clear, but I do not deny the speakability of the Cavander. The poeticism of the similes in the opening stanza gives a control to the tone of the ode that seems to me less moving than the more chaotic rendering in the Fitts, but that does not make the Cavander unspeakable or without a point of view. My only feeling is that the point of view is less primal, less basically human than the Fitts. Religious salvation is too surely hinted at. However, I can *see* the Cavander chorus, something I cannot do in Grene's version, a version whose meaning I like but whose tone of voice seems, to say the least, muddy.[3] Here is his opening stanza:

> What is the sweet spoken word of God from the shrine of Pytho rich
> in gold

3 David Grene and Richmond Lattimore, eds., *Sophocles I* (Modern Library, Random House, n.d.) .

that has come to glorious Thebes?
I am stretched on the rack of doubt, and terror and trembling hold
my heart, O Delian Healer, and I worship full of fears
for what doom you will bring to pass, new or renewed in the revolving
   years.
Speak to me, immortal voice,
child of golden Hope.

This is hard to speak, if for no other reason than the length of the sentences. It is simply harder to hear such an extension, since the voice cannot make its vocal emphases with anything like simple force. It is hard to get to the point in the Grene rendering. Such a withholding is feasible enough in a reading to oneself, where pause or rereading is possible. It is much more difficult to hold the focus of the thought in an oral delivery. What may, in the reading to one-self, give elaboration tends in the oral rendering to sound evasive at best, unintelligible at worst. The evasiveness might create a fawning kind of fear of God, a cringing, but I don't think the rest of the ode would support such a reading. It tends more to sound simply verbose and as a consequence less forceful in production.

The Cavander, whatever its limitations as to point of view (for me, it sounds more Christian than Greek, more sure of God's ways with human endeavor than is most Greek drama with which I am familiar), is nevertheless a playable statement, and it is with that feature that I am concerned. It seems to me that a view like Kitto's in his *Greek Tragedy* about Sophoclean choruses—namely, that they are affected by the action which surrounds them rather than being an objective, disinterested comment upon that action—not only is correct, but also demands some understanding of the chorus that will allow a director to move it, to give it a reason for speaking. I would imagine the movement for the two choruses here not at all similar. Though both are prayers, the more formulary quality of Cavander asks for more formulary movement. If we visualize some-place on the stage an altar (and since the play opens with sup-pliants, I would think an altar would be an essential part of the set), then some sense of prayer directed to that altar is probably called for in either translation. One would expect, however, a regularity of movement in the Cavander, a formality. I am perfectly aware that any movement is possible for any statement, thereby imposing upon the statement whatever mood or feeling one wishes to suggest. In other words, even given my reading of the Cavander translation, it is still possible for a director to choose to play against that reading. It might even be advantageous to do so. It is, after all, one of the primary ways theatre can achieve a certain sophistication. If a producer is aware of a tremendous control in the first seven or so lines of the Cavander, he may well wish to surround it with a sense of hysteria in order to suggest how tenuous, how inadequate the control is. The important thing here is to recognize the attempt at reasonable discourse that those similes suggest and to make use of it.

I can imagine a desperate attempt (in the Cavander translation) to escape Apollo's injunction after the Priest's exit prior to the ode, by some abortive attempt at exit on the part of the chorus or perhaps a huddling together in search of some kind of human support before beginning to speak. Speech is not always the first response to information that one does not quite understand or know what to do with. What the first lines of the ode suggest, however, is that by the time the chorus does speak, it has taken a position in regard to the information it has heard before the ode is begun. After some search of each other's faces for answers and probably some search of the altar, the physical representation of God, they seem to recognize their littleness, their inadequacy and, using their intelligence—the one thing that makes them perhaps more than dumb brutes—they state their condition as carefully as they can and address Apollo with the dignity of rationality. Their terror may be near hysteria, but it is at least tentatively under control. It is hard to imagine an honest reading of those first lines from twelve or fifteen bodies spread around the stage focused in different directions, in different physical positions which suggest different states of confusion. There is an agreement about how to face God, a sense of standing together, that is not suggested in the Fitts.

As one looks at Fitts' first strophe, I think he finds much less assurance about how to respond to Apollo's injunction here, much more fear and confusion. Through the "Fear unjoints me, the roots of my heart tremble," the Fitts chorus is still searching for a way to respond. Their hysteria, their despair, their inability to comprehend a way to respond are reflected in what they say. Their first statement is not a description of what has happened but a question, and a very basic question at that: What is God up to? And their first reaction to their inability to guess what he is up to is a fear that "unjoints" them. They have no notion of a correct stance in the face of the information they have received. Their first sense of where to look for an answer, and I should think their first discovery of the altar, that representation of God, is in their "Now I remember." Even here their sense of discovery of where to turn has none of the assurance or religious humility of the Cavander. At the climax of their discovery, their cry (and it is a cry not a statement) is a plea that can only hope for response. There is certainly no assurance in that "Speak, speak to us" and in that "be tender." How much calmer, more seemingly assured is Cavander's "only the child of golden hope, whose voice / Will never die, only the spirit of truth can tell us." There is no *absolute* assurance here, but neither is there any great fear toward whatever the answer might be.

The movement, then, in the Cavander seems to start with the chorus's admission to one another of their fear (the first five lines might well be addressed to one another to suggest their similarity in feeling). The next four are carefully addressed to Apollo (focused perhaps on the altar where they have found him or in the heavens where they feel sure he resides) to ask what he would have them do. The next two are a statement of their submission to his will whatever it may be (perhaps bowed heads would indicate that attitude). In the first four lines of the Fitts there are a greater number of attitudes expressed. There is first the question of what is going on, but it is divided into two parts, so that the chorus can turn comfortably in more than one direction in its search for an answer. And there is finally the first conclusion of that search: fear. There is no comfort here or hope, only a devastating fear that makes any rational answer impossible. Only after this, in their "Now I remember," is there a sense of somewhere to turn for comfort. Unlike the Cavander, in which the process of coming to terms with Apollo's injunction must appear in pre-speech pantomime, it is all here in the Fitts, all verbalized. Clearly the advantage to such spelling out in the words is the additional attitudes that can be projected in the movement. As the Fitts continues, Artemis and Athenê and again Apollo seem each to be a new hope, a new possibility for help, and the "O gods" in the first antistrophe, coming as it does in the middle of a sentence as if interrupting their plea to Apollo, has a desperate ring that is never heard in the almost listlike, ritualistic prayer in the Cavander. Everything in Cavander down to "Come now to help us" (line 21) is of the same tone. It is a humble, formulary plea that has little change of direction in it. It is a recognizable human attitude, but hardly a moving one. The Fitts reminds us continually of the terror of our humanity, not only our helplessness but our littleness, our desperateness.

What I wish to stress most is the dramatizable event in both translations. Unlike the lyrical, descriptive voice Grene gives us, there is something theatrical in these translations, something playable in typical theatrical terms. Neither the Fitts nor the Cavander translation is addressed to space. They both embody dramatic actions. They are not third-person descriptions of an event in which the chorus is not involved, as so many choruses appear to be as one watches them in production. Both choruses are Thebans caught in a plague that is destroying them. They are speaking not of Oedipus or the house of Laius but of themselves. It is their death and destruction they fear, and it is their search for salvation that forces this ode out of their mouths. They speak to themselves, they speak to God, they may (if a producer so wishes) speak to the audience; but they speak for themselves and of their own plight in precisely the same way Hamlet speaks of his in a soliloquy, or old Ephraim Cabot in Eugene O'Neill's *Desire Under the Elms* speaks to himself about the smell of the farm and its suggestion of unease. All of these characters have a problem they need to solve, and their verbalization of it is dramatic. It is perhaps difficult to think of the chorus as a single attitude, much like a single character, but it is completely misleading if one does not. The initial sense of leading the voice of this ode psychologically through the event being described and looking for the transitions that allow a human voice to get from one idea to the next is precisely the same as it would be if one were dealing with a single character in a play. It is still necessary to ask to whom one is speaking in the ode and to ask what the situation is that motivates that speech.

It is even valuable to ask such subtextual questions as where the chorus comes from; this ode is delivered after their entrance. What information have they, and where did they get it? Clearly they know about Apollo's edict; where did they get the information? They weren't on stage when Creon announced it. Have the priest and suppliants told them? Is it of any value to consider *them* the suppliants? Can one help present the immediacy of their concern by having them ask the priest that opening question as translated in the Fitts? If not, what is their relation to the priest and the suppliants? They are Theban Elders. Why? Of what importance is this fact to what they do and say and how they do and say it? It is, it seems to me, only by asking and answering such questions that we can have a meaningful modern production. If we assume simply that they are a chorus, something that always appears in Greek tragedy, and let it go at that, we can only at the very best get an imitation of a preconceived guess at what an imagined fifth-century Greek tragedy was like. I am not here arguing against the value of historical study; I am arguing against definitive dependence upon it. Its conclusions at best are only educated guesses, and for the most part guesses made by scholars educated as classicists or historians, not as theatre practitioners. Theatrical education tells us something about the way actors work and how they realize their performances. I am suggesting here that that knowledge be applied to all theatre, classic as well as modern. I think that throughout *Oedipus* such questions will help producers move a chorus and help a chorus speak with conviction.

Clearly their convictions in each ode are different, and I think that difference is dependent upon what has happened to them. Their conclusion in the second ode that Teiresias' accusation of Oedipus as the killer is a lie, that their "great lord" cannot be a criminal, is greatly qualified after Oedipus argues with Creon and sees his wife's dismissal of soothsayers shaken. They are searching for their own salvation, and their change in allegiance and in sympathy is at least in part an attempt to keep themselves away from catastrophe. And this attempt is echoed in the way they speak, qualified by the new information they possess.

Mainly in the interests of saving space, I will stay with the Fitts translation through the other odes. Let me stress, however, that the Cavander chorus continues to have a point of view. Throughout the play, the chorus is more sure of God's final justice; they are more positive that the world is rational. In the second ode, they speak not only of the murderer who must be hunted but also of their fear of Teiresias' accusation of Oedipus, an accusation so monstrous that it shakes their conviction of a rational world. This is the beginning of the Cavander translation:

> The wisdom of the priest sets fear, fear, beating in our blood;
> Truth or lies, nothing comforts, nothing denies.
> The world is built out of our beliefs,
> And when we lose those beliefs in doubt,
> Our world is destroyed, and the present and the past
> Vanish into night.

They hold tightly to their conviction that a life led within modest limits is blameless and will go unpunished. In a startling difference from Jebb, Grene, and Fitts, Cavander not only says, in the last verse of this ode, that God is wise and man may be fallible but goes the strange step further, suggested in none of the other texts, that man may protect himself against his own fallibility by prayer:

> Yet wisdom may come to us, not the wisdom that sees
> How the world is ruled, but the wisdom that guides
> The modest life. In this alone we may excel.

Compare Fitts, whose translation of the same lines is:

> No man can judge that rough unknown or trust in second sight,
> For wisdom changes hands among the wise.

How unsure Fitts is of the power of man's wisdom! The Cavander chorus is firmly convinced of the justice, the order of the world, and this they will hang onto at all costs. In the next ode, for example, where God's injunctions in the oracle are in question, the Cavander chorus is absolute in its insistence that God's utterances make sense:

> The temple of Zeus, and Olympia, command our prayers;
> But we shall never believe again
> Until the truth of this murder is known.
> Let us be sure of our beliefs, give us proof.

And when all is solved, although they admit their love, their respect for Oedipus, they cannot help but point out that "Oedipus aimed beyond the reach of man / And fixed with his arrowing mind / Perfection and rich happiness." One is again reminded of the possibility of a right way and a wrong way, and the chorus is convinced, as I fear we are asked to be, of the existence of the former.

The Fitts chorus continues to be less sure of how the world works.

They want it to make sense, but they are more emotionally aware of the difficulty in being sure. Perhaps a better way to put it is that they are more emotionally motivated:

The Delphic stone of prophecies   STROPHE 1
Remembers ancient regicide
And a still bloody hand.
That killer's hour of flight has come.
He must be stronger than riderless
Coursers of untiring wind.
For the son of Zeus armed with his father's thunder
Leaps in lightning after him;
And the Furies follow him, the sad Furies.

Holy Parnassos' peak of snow   ANTISTROPHE 1
Flashes and blinds that secret man,
That all shall hunt him down:
Though he may roam the forest shade
Like a bull gone wild from pasture
To rage through glooms of stone.
Doom comes down on him; flight will not avail him;
For the world's heart calls him desolate,
And the immortal Furies follow, for ever follow.

But now a wilder thing is heard   STROPHE 2
From the old man skilled at hearing Fate in the wingbeat of
    a bird.
Bewildered as a blown bird, my soul hovers and cannot find
Foothold in this debate, or any reason or rest of mind.
But no man ever brought—none can bring
Proof of strife between Thebes' royal house,
Labdakos' line, and the son of Polybos;
And never until now has any man brought word
Of Laios' dark death staining Oedipus the King.

Divine Zeus and Apollo hold   ANTISTROPHE 2
Perfect intelligence alone of all tales ever told;
And well though this diviner works, he works in his own
    night;
No man can judge that rough unknown or trust in
    second sight,
For wisdom changes hands among the wise.
Shall I believe my great lord criminal
At a raging word that a blind old man let fall?
I saw him, when the carrion woman faced him of old,
Prove his heroic mind! These evil words are lies.

They respond less like a group of holy brothers comfortable in their convictions and more like a group in search, grasping at appearances and trying their best to understand them. What happens in Thebes is not a demonstration of the way the world works, but a fact that must be somehow dealt with in their tentative struggle at structuring that world. They are sure of the Delphic oracle and its naming the killer of Laius (whoever he may be) as the cause of their suffering. It is with anger and assurance that they start that second ode:

> The Delphic stone of prophecies
> Remembers ancient regicide
> And a still bloody hand.
> That killer's hour of flight has come.

The tetrameter, even broken as it is in the third line, gives an almost martial quality to their conviction as they tell us and one another of their reaction to the announcement. How different this metrical assurance from the opening lines of the Parados. And the first strophe and antistrophe continue this metric pattern. It is only in the second strophe that the meter modulates—strangely, I must admit, but truly nonetheless. Fitts chooses to run his tetrameter lines together, which makes for a different reading, a more flowing, less final beat to the end of each line. What might logically follow the first two verses in metric structure as

> But now a wilder thing is heard
> From the old man skilled at hearing Fate
> In the wingbeat of a bird.
> Bewildered as a blown bird,
> My soul hovers and cannot find
> Foothold in this debate,
> Or any reason or rest of mind.

becomes

> But now a wilder thing is heard
> From the old man skilled at hearing Fate in the wingbeat of a bird.
> Bewildered as a blown bird, my soul hovers and cannot find
> Foothold in this debate, or any reason or rest of mind.

Such a shift makes for a different reading. The line-end pauses are now in the middle of a line, and we must push past what might be a normal line-end caesura. Such a reading suggests a sense of bewilderment. The chorus as they react to the accusation of Oedipus as the killer of Laius is less comfortable, less sure. They are afraid, not so much that their philosophical convictions are in doubt, but that their king is a murderer and therefore that their immediate day-to-day life may be subject to horrifying change. It is, I think, a much more public and theatrical demonstration of fear than the Cavander. We are not here worried about a philosophical conviction but a world. States topple, not ideas; and in theatre the former collapse is generally more theatrically realizable. It is difficult, for example, to know how to show the intellectual spiritual change in T. S. Eliot's Beckett in *Murder in the Cathedral*—that "Now I see, now is my way clear . . . ," his last speech in Part I—since whatever caused it took place in his head, not on the stage. Even all the offstage voices of priests and tempters don't altogether accomplish or demonstrate that change theatrically. So here, it seems to me, we are more immediately connected to a human, public attitude that is dramatizable. And the ode ends not with a comment on the way man can live the modest life in some sense of safety, but in a question about their king's guilt, a guilt they cannot at this point be sure of. Their concern is not about their own moral convictions but about the world they immediately live in and how it works.

I am also struck by the focus with which the ode begins in Fitts. One can imagine the chorus turning to the altar and addressing it as a reflection of that Delphic stone. Somehow the Delphic stone suggests the altar more immediately than Cavander's "In the rock at Delphi there is a cave." The militant, organized fear through the first two stanzas asks for a directed focus to some representation of God. There is an attitude suggested by the regular cadence of the Fitts which can be visualized, and while that attitude might be construed out of the Cavander, it is not suggested by it. My own preference would be a uniform movement by the chorus toward the altar with whatever ritual in that movement that might best demonstrate the chorus's recognition of the oracle's awesome power. That regular pulse which is inherent in the verse lets us know this. Similarly, the break in the second strophe suggests a new movement, a different response. Here, rather than a regularity of unified conviction, the more lyrical flow implies a more fearful, less sure attitude, as if they were talking to one another, or at least to something other than the recognized authority of Delphi they are questioning. The "wilder thing" is not something that can be bowed to or easily accepted, and the verse suggests that change. The chorus turns from God and his representation in the altar, perhaps from their focus above them, to "Holy Parnassos' peak of snow," to their own unsureness. And whether that is visualized by their search for answers in each other or merely by a less unified look to God, the verse certainly shows some change in focus, something less sure in attitude.

Fitts gives us their unsureness and lets us as directors (or actors or producers) visualize it, just as in the second antistrophe he gives us their resolution. It is a quiet resolution, it has none of the pounding, fearful, emotional assurance of the opening, but it allows them to go on, to continue their search for salvation. God has mentioned a killer, only Teiresias has said that the killer is Oedipus, and after all Teiresias is only a man. There is still the possibility of solution for their devastation without the destruction of the hero who has been their salvation before: "I saw him, when the carrion woman faced him of old, / Prove his heroic mind! These evil words are lies." It is a fascinating exposé of the helpless human desire for salvation, for a way to live—their admission of the power of divinity, or at least some inexplicable force in the world that creates their problems, and at the same time their trust in the human power to deal with it. They never question God, but they must from their own human limitations (and it is the best in such limitations that Oedipus represents) find some way to cope with what God brings them. Even in the next ode, an ode in which the chorus openly questions the validity of the gods, the worry of the chorus is the collapse of reverence in their leaders, their fear that Oedipus, their *sacred* king (my emphasis), may not be reverent.[4]

I think throughout his translation, Fitts reminds us of something that I have perhaps not made enough of. When Corrigan speaks of language that is "eminently actable," he is really defending the prosaic and more naturalistic speech of the Cavander. His claim, in

[4] In other translations, almost without exception, the burden of the chorus's concern is not the lack of reverence in their masters but the fear that the oracle, the voice of God, may be wrong and therefore their worship foolish. I cannot argue for Fitts' interpretation of the Greek, but his own emphasis on the position that authority (Oedipus) must take makes the focus of the chorus much more a part of the drama taking place.

that "Note on the Translation" from which I quoted earlier, that the rhythms of Cavander's verse are "smooth and consistent with the play's inner action; they are natural without being naturalistic" is lovely, but unfortunately it isn't true. None of Cavander's verses creates a poetic form of any kind; it is only in the wildest sense that there are line ends even suggesting verse, and if we look closely at these ends, we are struck by no metrical pattern either of beat or foot that let us hear something as formal as verse. His language is clear, but it is not very good poetry.

Now, good poetry is harder to speak well; it is also more precise in what it says. We should not take the simplest or clearest surface statement of what is happening as necessarily the best rendering of what is happening. Our concern in drama is not only with what happens but with characters' reactions to what happens, and their reactions are defined by the way they speak. We hear their tone of voice by the way a translator uses language, just as we judge our friends' and colleagues' convictions by the way they phrase them. The fact that someone says something is real for him tells us nothing about the sophistication of the view, the intelligence of the conviction, or the worth of the statement. We make these judgments on the *way* he expresses the truth.

So here language tells us not only what the choric reaction is to an event but how that chorus feels about it. The chorus may simply tell us what has happened—certainly, that is the first function of the first ode—they may also tell us how they feel about what has happened, and this latter concern is the greatest concern of the producer and, one would hope, a major concern for the translator. Clarity cannot be too simply come by, especially in Greek tragedy. It may simply belittle the importance of what that tragedy has to say. And equally important, it may make unclear to whom and about what exactly that tragedy is speaking. The continual problem for directors in making the chorus a meaningful part of the play they are producing is to know, or at least to be able to guess, the answers to these questions. The use of language is the clearest cue they have.

I have been speaking, in my discussion of *Oedipus,* primarily of the direction or focus of the choric speeches and the tone of their concern, but often the very action of a play is shaped by the way

CHAPTER II

choric speeches are phrased. I want to quote two translations of the first ode in *The Bacchae* by Euripides. This is the entrance ode of the Bacchantes, the followers of Dionysus, and in it they announce their intention of singing the "old hymn to Dionysus." By this announcement we have some idea of the event. It is to be, at the very least, an expression of their feelings about their God, but only the verbal structure itself can suggest the form that that song might take. Here is the Vellacott translation:[5]

> From far-off lands of Asia,
> From Tmolus the holy mountain,
> We run with the god of laughter;
> Labour is joy and weariness is sweet,
> And our song resounds to Bacchus!
>
> Beware of the interloper!
> Indoors or out, who listens?
> Let every lip be holy;
> Stand well aloof, be silent, while we sing
> The appointed hymn to Bacchus!
>
> Blest is the happy man
> Who knows the mysteries the gods ordain,
> And sanctifies his life,
> And steeps his soul in holy revelry,
> And, by due ritual made pure,
> Enters the ecstasy of mountain solitudes;
> Who observes the mystic rites
> Made lawful by Cybele the Great Mother;
> Who crowns his head with ivy,
> And shakes aloft his wand in worship of Dionysus.
>
> On, on! Run, dance, delirious, possessed!
> Dionysus comes to his own;
> Bring from the Phrygian hills to the broad streets of Hellas
> The god, child of a god,
> Spirit of revel and rapture, Dionysus!
>
> Once, on the womb that held him
> The fire-bolt flew from the hand of Zeus;
> And pains of child-birth bound his mother fast,
> And she cast him forth untimely,
> And under the lightning's lash relinquished life;

[5] Philip Vellacott, trans., *Euripides: The Bacchae and Other Plays* (Penguin Books, 1954).

And Zeus the son of Cronos
Ensconced him instantly in the secret womb
Chambered within his thigh,
And with golden pins closed him from Hera's sight.

So, when the Fates had made him ripe for birth,
Zeus bore the bull-horned god
And wreathed his head with wreaths of writhing snakes;
Which is why the Maenads catch
Wild snakes, nurse them and twine them round their hair.

O Thebes, old nurse that cradled Semele,
Be ivy-garlanded, burst into flower
With wreaths of lush bright-berried bryony,
Bring sprays of fir, green branches torn from oaks,
Fill soul and flesh with Bacchus' mystic power;
Fringe and bedeck your dappled fawnskin cloaks
With wooly tufts and locks of purest white.
There is a brute wildness in the fennel-wands—
Reverence it well. Soon the whole land will dance
   When the god with ecstatic shout
   Leads his companies out
   To the mountain's mounting height
   Swarming with riotous bands
   Of Theban women leaving
   Their spinning and their weaving
   Stung with the maddening trance
     Of Dionysus!

O secret chamber the Curetes knew!
O holy cavern in the Cretan glade
Where Zeus was cradled, where for our delight
The triple-crested Corybantes drew
Tight the round drum-skin, till its wild beat made
Rapturous rhythm to the breathing sweetness
Of Phrygian flutes! Then divine Rhea found
The drum could give her Bacchic airs completeness;
   From her, the Mother of all,
   The crazy Satyrs seen,
   In their dancing festival
   When the second year comes round,
   Seized on the Timbrel's tune
   To play the leading part
   In feasts that delight the heart
     Of Dionysus.

O what delight is in the mountains!
There the celebrant, wrapped in his sacred fawnskin,
Flings himself on the ground surrendered,

While the swift-footed company streams on;
There he hunts for blood, and rapturously
Eats the raw flesh of the slaughtered goat,
Hurrying on to the Phrygian or Lydian mountain heights.
Possessed, ecstatic, he leads their happy cries;
The earth flows with milk, flows with wine,
Flows with nectar of bees;
The air is thick with a scent of Syrian myrrh.
The celebrant runs entranced, whirling the torch
That blazes red from the fennel-wand in his grasp,
And with shouts he rouses the scattered bands,
Sets their feet dancing,
As he shakes his delicate leeks to the wild wind.
And amidst the frenzy of song he shouts like thunder:
'On, on! Run, dance, delirious, possessed!
You, the beauty and grace of golden Tmolus,
Sing to the rattle of thunderous drums,
Sing for joy,
Praise Dionysus, god of joy!
Shout like Phrygians, sing out the tunes you know,
While the sacred pure-toned flute
Vibrates the air with holy merriment,
In time with the pulse of the feet that flock
To the mountains, to the mountains!'
And every daughter of Bacchus runs and leaps for joy,
Like a foal with its mother at pasture.

Here is the Arrowsmith translation:[6]

Out of the land of Asia,
down from holy Tmolus,
speeding the service of god,
for Bromius we come!
Hard are the labours of god,
hard, but his service is sweet.
Sweet to serve, sweet to cry:
    Bacchus! Evohé!

—You on the streets!
                —You on the roads!
                                —Make way!

—Let every mouth be hushed. Let no ill-omened words profane
    your tongues.
                —Make way! Fall back!

6 William Arrowsmith, trans., *The Bacchae,* in David Grene and Richmond
Lattimore, eds., *The Complete Greek Tragedies: Euripides V* (University of
Chicago Press, 1959) .

—For now raise the old, old hymn to Dionysus,
—Blessèd, blessèd are those who know the mysteries of god.
—Blessèd is he who hallows his life in the worship of god, he whom the
    spirit of god possesseth, who is one with those who belong to the
    holy body of god,
—Blessèd are the dancers and those who are purified, who dance on the
    hill in the holy dance of god.
—Blessèd are they who keep the rite of Cybele the Mother.
—Blessèd are the thyrsus bearers those who wield in their hands the
    holy wand of god,
—Blessèd are those who wear the crown of the ivy of god.
—Blessèd, blessèd are they; Dionysus is their god!

—On, Bacchae, on, you Bacchae,
  bear your god in triumph home!
  Bear on the God, son of god,
  escort your Dionysus home!
  Bear him down from Phrygian hill,
  attend him through the streets of Hellas!

—So his mother bore him once
  in labor bitter; lightning-struck,
  forced by fire that flared from Zeus,
  consumed, she died, untimely torn,
  in childbed dead by blow of light!
  Of light the son was born!

—Zeus it was who saved his son;
  with speed outrunning mortal eye,
  bore him to a private place,
  bound the boy with clasps of gold;
  in his thigh as in a womb,
  concealed his son from Hera's eyes.

—And when the weaving Fates fulfilled the time,
  the bull-horned god was born of Zeus. In joy
  he crowned his son, set serpents on his head—
  wherefrom, in piety, descends to us
  the Maenad's writhing crown, her *chevelure* of snakes.

—O Thebes, nurse of Semele,
  crown your hair with ivy!
  Grow green with bryony!
  Redden with berries! O city,
  with boughs of oak and fir,
  come dance the dance of god!
  Fringe your skins of dappled fawn
  with tufts of twisted wool!
  Handle with holy care
  the violent wand of god!

CHAPTER II

And let the dance begin!
He is Bromius who runs
to the mountain!
                to the mountain!
where the throng of women waits,
driven from shuttle and loom,
possessed by Dionysus!

—And I praise the holies of Crete,
the caves of the dancing Curetes,
there where Zeus was born,
where helmed in triple tier
around the primal drum
the Corybantes danced. They,
they were the first of all
whose whirling feet kept time
to the strict beat of the taut hide
and the squeal of the wailing flute.
Then from them to Rhea's hands
the holy drum was handed down;
but, stolen by the raving Satyrs,
fell at last to me and now
accompanies the dance
which every other year
celebrates your name:
    Dionysus!

—He is sweet upon the mountains. He drops to the earth from the
    running packs.
He wears the holy fawn-skin. He hunts the wild goat and kills it.
He delights in the raw flesh.
He runs to the mountains of Phrygia, to the mountain of Lydia he runs!
He is Bromius who leads us! *Evohé!*

—With milk the earth flows! It flows with wine!
It runs with the nectar of bees!

—Like frankincense in its fragrance
is the blaze of the torch he bears.
Flames float out from his trailing wand
    as he runs, as he dances,
    kindling the stragglers,
    spurring with cries,
and his long curls stream to the wind!

—And he cries, as they cry, *Evohé!*—
    On, Bacchae!
    On, Bacchae!
Follow, glory of golden Tmolus,
    hymning god

with a rumble of drums,
with a cry, *Evohé!* to the Evian god,
with a cry of Phrygian cries,
when the holy flute like honey plays
the sacred song of those who go
to the mountain!
> *to the mountain!*

—Then, in ecstasy, like a colt by its grazing mother, the Bacchante runs
with flying feet, she leaps!

It is, first of all, very difficult to tell exactly what, more than a description of the Bacchic worship as contained in their "appointed hymn," is going on in the Vellacott translation. One might guess that the fourth stanza, beginning "On, on! Run, dance, delirious, possessed," is not part of the hymn, but one is given no particular hint by a change in verse form or rhythm as to what that change means. We are fairly certain by the time we come to the seventh stanza, beginning "O Thebes, old nurse," that we are not in the hymn, since the Bacchae are not addressing Thebes, the land they have just arrived in, not yet a land of believers, and hardly, one would expect, to be referred to in the "appointed hymn." But even here the shift to a new focus of address seems to be muddied by the repeated use of "O" in the succeeding stanzas. Both of the succeeding verses start with that "O," as if they were still descriptions of the Bacchic frenzy. To be sure, the excitement increases, the description becomes more intense, but even this increase of intensity is controlled. When we come to, or at least toward, the climax of the chorus some twelve lines from the end and hear "On, on! Run, dance, delirious, possessed," we remember that the identical line in a similar metric context has already appeared to introduce the fourth stanza of the chorus. Just as an actable event, then, the ode gives us a hymn which increases in intensity from "Blest is the happy man" to "Wild snakes, nurse them and twine them round their hair." It is possible that the seeming frenzy of the first "On, on! Run, dance, delirious, possessed," which begins the fourth stanza, might be something other than the hymn, but it is certainly not clear what. Nowhere in the chorus is it suggested, either by a sharp change of tone or verse form or meter, that more than a description of the Dionysiac worship is operating here.

The Arrowsmith version, accurately or inaccurately, gives us a great deal more and forces the director to something much more explicit, however he finally chooses to present it. The ode is clearly divided into six sections. First there is the Bacchantes' announcement of who they are and where they are from, a section nicely ended with the shout *"Bacchus! Evohé!"* Next they command outsiders to "Make way! Fall back!" while they sing their hymn to Dionysus. How different this announcement and authoritative command from the two-verse announcement in Vellacott—an announcement that could be construed to do what the Arrowsmith translation does, but need not. In fact, it would not surprise one if the division were missed in production. The third section in the Arrowsmith is the hymn, very clearly set off by the beatitude-like prayer which becomes a single unit through the repetition at the beginning of each line of "Blessèd" and the long irregular meter of the lines, their similarity being made clear by the repetition at the beginning of each line. How sharply differentiated metrically is this section from the next, which runs from "On, Bacchae, on, you Bacchae" to *"chevelure* of snakes." The first three stanzas here are all tetrameter lines, and the martial or at least processional quality of the verse is very hard to ignore. This is particularly true in light of the opening command, "On, Bacchae, on, you Bacchae, / bear your god in triumph home!" Some procession is suggested, and when one looks at the subject matter of the stanzas in question, it is not a difficult jump to assume a ceremony that recreates the birth of Dionysus. Actually, I think the ceremony, the ritual ceremony of the birth of Dionysus enacted in whatever way the director visualizes such a ritual, goes through the next verse and does not end until we come to "O Thebes." The change in meter from the more martial tetrameter to the longer, pentameter line is like a softening, a quieting within the ceremony itself. The stanza brings us to a peaceful conclusion of the ceremony, a birth surrounded by reverential worshippers wearing their wreath of piety, that *chevelure* of snakes. To be sure, the wreath is not what one might expect as a representation of reverence; but as we are to find out in the play, it is an unusual religion—at once reverential and bestial.

This ceremony, generally a quiet one, I think, not ecstatic, ends, and the chorus (in the Arrowsmith translation) exhorts Thebes, a land as yet uninitiated to the rites of Dionysus, a land to which Dionysus has brought his followers specifically *to* initiate the Thebans, to join their chorus, their band of Bacchantes. The next stanza, with its reference to the "primal drum" around which the "Corybantes danced," where the "whirling feet kept time / to the strict beat of the taut hide / and the squeal of the wailing flute," seems to be a preparation for the truly ecstatic climax to the chorus, and one assumes to the religious worship itself which begins in the almost free-verse excitement of what I see as the celebration of the ecstasy of Bacchic worship, the kind of "out of mind" commitment the two messengers are to describe as having seen later in the play. It may be hard to dance to this and describe it at the same time, but I think some members of the chorus at least must dance it, or at least show in their movements the kind of excitement that is here described. The description is so immediate, the rhythms so insistent, that a simple recitation of the lines does not do enough to recreate their excitement. I am sure that a creative drummer improvising around an intelligent reading of these last stanzas could suggest the kind of physical excitement that is inherent in the lines. The duple metric feeling is not obvious, but it is there as a base for just such improvisation.

What started out as a discussion of how to understand and incorporate a chorus into a production of a Greek tragedy may seem to have turned into a discussion of translations. If so, it is perhaps necessary. All we have as a real basis for modern production of any classical play is the translation. All discussion of performances are at best secondhand and generally little more than educated guesses. Discussions of costumes, of *cothurnus* and *onkos,* of raised loggia or orchestra-level loggia, even of dance and music, are only general descriptions of what actors might have appeared in and where they might have appeared. No such discussion can ever recreate the tragedy with the kind of power it often has in the reading. It is possible to have a pseudo-historical recreation (I say pseudo because it can never, for certain, be exact), but the modern producer's concern is to present what moves him in the play in a way that might move an audience the same way. He will certainly use historical backgrounds and research, but his production must recreate the text in modern parallels in which the audience can recognize its own experience.

CHAPTER II

It is through translations, then, the tone of voice, the exposing of what the action might be, the way characters see one another, that we must come to terms with the text. This is as true of the chorus as of the principals, and I have dealt with only the chorus here, in hopes that some sense of how they might operate in a play can be suggested by the way they speak, by the way the translator sees them as actors in a play. Nor do I think the particular odes I have dealt with here are in any way unusual or different from most odes in tragedy. The great climactic ode in *Oedipus* that I have not mentioned earlier, the ode that begins in the Fitts translation "Alas for the seed of men," presents similar but not more unsolvable problems than the earlier odes. If anything, it is easier to work with since its despair and the immediate reference of that despair to "the seed of men," which includes the chorus, makes the chorus more a participant in the horror of Oedipus' collapse than do preceding odes. So too, in *The Bacchae,* the other choruses are not so dramatic in what they depict, but there is always a suggestion of their relation to the main action. In fact, generally the Euripidean chorus seems to me more obviously a part of the organic movement of the play. It is, after all, the Trojan women who concern us in that play, not just the voices of Hecuba and Andromache, and even the old women of Troezen in *Hippolytus* are more immediately involved with Phaedra and the nurse than the old men in *Oedipus* are with the king. The Bacchantes are a continual and necessary reminder of what Dionysus is urging Pentheus and Agave toward, both what is pleasurable and what is disastrous. And though the odes are a continual comment on the action they follow, they are also manifestations of what the Bacchae are and what the Dionysian religion is.

What I have been talking about, however, is a general way language works in plays, the way it tells us what the event described by language is and how it may be presented to us. Insofar as the chorus has had a point of view, I have tried to examine it, but because their view is less that of a personality and more that of a society, my remarks necessarily have concerned themselves with that larger issue. The personal problem was not yet of interest to the playwright. Regardless of the hints of such a concern in Euripides, it is not a real one for most students of drama, until we get to Marlowe and Shakespeare. Everyman's concerns in the play of that name are still every man's. Faustus begins to get more particular. And Hamlet's problems are those of a very particular individual indeed. Give Othello Hamlet's problems, for example, and there is no tragedy. The particularity of personality is vital here to the catastrophe that overtakes it.

CHAPTER II

III

Subtexts in Shakespeare

It seems to me that American actors and directors are afraid of Shakespeare, or at least treat him as if he were a different breed of playwright from Tennessee Williams and Arthur Miller. I don't think he is. I think a fairly convincing case can be made to show that all three playwrights use language to define characters. Williams and Miller use language in such a comparatively simple fashion that their characters are fairly clear-cut. Furthermore, because neither uses language with the same precision that Shakespeare does and because the characterizations are close to our own time and society, it is easy for American actors to fill out a Willy Loman or a Blanche DuBois. We tend to think of Hamlet or Lady Macbeth as something foreign, unreal, and hence in need of some creative approach other than that used in finding Willy or Blanche. I really can see no reason why we should think so.

The problem with Shakespeare is not that there is no consistent psychology in his creations, but that the psychology is a good deal more subtle and sophisticated than that given us by Williams or Miller. It may take a greater imaginative leap to create a Lear than a Loman, but in both cases the leap is to the creation of a fiction that makes psychological sense to the actor. It is true that one must know a good deal about how rhyme and rhythm, how poetic form in fact, create the tone of voice that an actor must finally fill out. And because the tone of voice is not simply hinted at, but given in language, a good deal more attention must be paid to the implications of language in good poetic drama than in Williams or Miller, or Eugene O'Neill. In O'Neill or Williams we often hear such a slight outline of human attitude that our job is necessarily filling it out; whereas in Shakespeare so much is given that our job is often only to realize what is there.

Modern drama is defined, at least in part, by its attempt to characterize, that is, to create attitudes that reflect less than the author's full intelligence. As it tries to create the common man, it also tends to create his limitations. Hence much of what makes him interesting is between the lines rather than in them, or more clearly it is the poses, the postures he puts on to cope with his problems that interest us rather than his best-articulated intelligence. If we look at the two tragic protagonists Blanche DuBois and Willy Loman, it is interesting to note how seldom we hear them speak with any sophisticated intelligence. Willy's most touching moments are in his imaginary dialogues with Ben or in his obviously lopsided observations to Biff about being liked or well-liked. We are touched, not by the exactness with which he sees his situation, but by his inability to see the world he lives in. It is not the fact that he is wrong that touches us, but that he is incapable of being either consciously wrong or right. He is trapped by his own inadequacies. This condition is very different from that of Macbeth; he too is wrong, but he is perfectly aware of the dangers of his wrongness and willing to chance them. In Willy it is the limitations of the man, the particularity of his problem, the *character*, that interests us.

Even in Willy's wife, it is the inadequacy of her great cry "Attention, attention must be paid to such a person" that moves us. We may pity Linda; we do not, in Aristotle's word, feel "fear." She is not one "like ourselves" as Lear, as Macbeth, even as Lady Macbeth is. Even her last speech in the play is an inadequate response to what has happened to her:

Forgive me, dear. I can't cry. I don't know what it is, but I can't cry. I don't understand it. Why did you ever do that? Help me, Willy, I can't cry. It seems to me that you're just on another trip. I keep expecting you. Willy, dear, I can't cry. Why did you do it? I search and search and I search and I can't understand it, Willy. I made the last payment on the house today. Today, dear. And there'll be nobody home. We're free and clear. We're free. We're free . . . We're free.

It is a touching speech, but its general burden is "I don't understand." One does not need intelligence to recreate the attitude, at least not to understand it. What is felt may be very complex (perhaps this is the reason for the tremendous concentration on releasing and communicating feeling in so much actor training today), but what is said is very simple. The emotional underpinnings may be highly sophisticated; the intelligence that must be heard most certainly is not. Even Biff, perhaps the most intelligent voice in the play, is terribly simplistic in his attempts to understand himself or get through to his father:

I ran down eleven flights with a pen in my hand today. And suddenly I stopped, you hear me? And in the middle of that office building, do you hear this? I stopped in the middle of that building and I saw—the sky. I saw the things that I love in this world. The work and the food and time to sit and smoke. And I looked at the pen and said to myself, what the hell am I grabbing this for? Why am I trying to become what I don't want to be? What am I doing in an office, making a contemptuous, begging fool of myself, when all I want is out there, waiting for me the minute I say I know who I am! Why can't I say that, Willy?   [Act II]

The repetitions, the continued questions, the simplicity of "I saw—the sky" are moving, but as reflections of emotional naïveté—not as expressions of an intelligent or in any way sophisticated mind.

Such limitation is not unique in Miller's drama. Blanche DuBois (in fact, most of Williams' heroes or heroines—Brick in *Cat on a Hot Tin Roof*, Val in *Orpheus Descending*, and the prototype for all of them, Laura in *The Glass Menagerie*, to name only the most obvious) is not so much limited intellectually as she is psychically crippled. Even more than Willy, she is a case study, one in fact who is finally taken away. It is interesting how far modern drama has gone in asking sympathy for our misfits—not misfits like Hamlet or Lear or Othello, misfits whose human limitations make them incapable of acting in the particular situation in which they find themselves, but misfits who are incapable of acting in the world at all—in any situation. Perhaps this accounts for our need to cast so much against type, to cast for those qualities in the actor that the author has not given the character in the script. Hence the need for a powerful Blanche rather than the broken thing she reads as, or a virile Paul Newman for the seemingly effeminate Brick. Part of the actor's job is to create what isn't verbally articulated.

In Shakespeare the job is invariably to realize what is verbally articulated. How different the kind of hysteria one hears in Blanche and Willy from the hysteria in Lear or Macbeth. In the latter cases the hysteria is of extreme awareness not total collapse. Macbeth may see that his life has fallen into "the sere, the yellow leaf," but he does not "depend on the kindness of strangers." He will die "with harness on [his] back." If Lear chooses to live in prison knowing that he is a "foolish fond old man," it is because he recognizes the real truth of the transience of human success, that it is possible to "wear out, / In a walled prison, packs and sets of great ones / That ebb and flow by the moon." And though it may be that he dies on an illusion, the illusion that Cordelia lives, that is not an illusion about what is important in life, about what makes it worth living, as Willy's suicide is. In Blanche and Willy we see case studies, characters who don't have possession of their best faculties; in Macbeth and Lear we see human convictions tested with all the intelligence that Shakespeare could bring to bear upon them. It is because of this intelligence that we must listen to what Lear says, whereas Willy's words are of minor importance. It is a particular kind of limited characterization that Miller wishes to show us. He does not need poetry or even very careful prose, since the ideas he wishes to articulate frame a quite simple attitude, a limited one.

Character, as I use it here, is the formation of a unique set of attitudes that are special to the culture or the period from which it comes. The nineteenth century flooded the stage with romantic heroes and villains whose greatest appeal was their size, their larger-than-society-could-hold conceits. They were heroes in the more ancient sense because they broke the bonds of social norms. Most of such creations are now forgotten, but even those we remember, those of Schiller and even Coleridge, are remembered not for their universality but their uniqueness, as outlaws, as men standing against society, just as today our heroes are smaller than life-size and are uniquely destroyed by society. They have less intelligence, fewer tools with which to face life, than most of us. They remind us of the pathetic She tragedies of the late seventeenth century to whose heroines we give pity, but little else. Character, in this sense, does not exist in Shakespeare. He puts highly sophisticated attitudes into difficult situations; as a consequence, we watch intelligent men try with all their power to cope with these situations. They are not limited by time or place, or social conditions, or a fuzzy intelligence. Their only limitations are in being human beings rather than gods. In this respect they are like the great tragic heroes of Greek tragedy.[1] Now, clearly, if we are to realize such giants, we need to recognize all the elements of poetry that go to make them up, to include those elements in our whole concept of subtext in creation. One of the necessities for a Shakespearean actor is an education. He simply cannot realize a Lear or a Macbeth if he does not understand the poetry that creates them.

That is not, I think, all an actor needs, but it is important; and it is certainly a defensible reason for the seemingly clichéd conviction that all an actor needs in order to play Shakespeare is a voice, a body, and an understanding of how to read poetry. It probably underlies Michael Redgrave's remark about Stanislavsky's method in preparing Shakespeare, that "the approach is not appropriate to the plays of Shakespeare who is more impressionist than realist." And Mr. Redgrave is no mean opponent, especially when, as here, he makes his case through Prospero in *The Tempest*.[2] I think he is wrong. Such an insistence leads to mad Ophelias who arrive on stage with mannered bedlam but no idea of the scene and to boring Prosperos with no motivation to speak their essentially expository and hence boring opening speech of forty minutes. Some attention to a subtextual reason for talking at such length, or even a not so subtextual but hardly poetic reason as a very real and apparent fury at his brother Antonio, might keep not only Miranda but the audience awake.

I can, however, understand Mr. Redgrave's worries. I think there are other attentions to be paid than to poetry, but certainly the prosified, "methody" American characterization is enough to give one pause. To believe, as many American actors seem to, that Shakespeare created characters and then embellished them with a poetry that could be thrown away once the character was found (I remember Donald Madden's Hotspur in such a context) is as least

---

[1] As I hope is clear from my earlier remarks on Greek tragedy, I think there is as much to be said about the way character is used by Shakespeare as against Sophocles as there is to compare Miller's use to Shakespeare. If Willy Loman seems more a particularized set of characteristics than Lear, so too Lear is easily that much more a particularized set of characteristics than Oedipus. There is something almost totally characterless about Oedipus—which is one of the reasons (Oedipus complex to the contrary) that actors have trouble holding onto that attitude in the kinds of psychological ways that are available in Shakespeare.

[2] Michael Redgrave, *The Actor's Ways and Means* (Heinemann, 1953), pp. 72–73.

as disastrous as the more British tendency to find the poetry and let the character go. In the first case, we have a modern rewriting of the plays filled with energetic but uneducated princes; in the second, a historical version that may echo a prince of the past but has little sense of an immediate human being. In the latter production Ophelia is clearly pathetic; in the former she is clearly mad. In neither version can one guess what she is doing on stage or why she is doing it.

Certainly before one tackles the problem of how to present the attitudes that Shakespeare has given us, one must know what the attitudes are. It is here that a real knowledge of how poetry or language creates attitude can tell us what, as actors, we must project. Let me quote Hamlet's first soliloquy and see what he is talking about and how Shakespeare has let us know his point of view toward what he is talking about:

> O that this too too sullied flesh would melt,
> Thaw and resolve itself into a dew!
> O that the Everlasting had not fix'd
> His canon 'gainst self-slaughter! O God! God!
> How weary, stale, flat, and unprofitable
> Seem to me all the uses of this world.
> Fie on't! ah fie! 'tis an unweeded garden,
> That grows to seed; things rank and gross in nature
> Possess it merely. That it should come to this!
> But two months dead: nay, not so much, not two:
> So excellent a king; that was, to this,
> Hyperion to a satyr; so loving to my mother
> That he might not beteem the winds of heaven
> Visit her face too roughly. Heaven and earth!
> Must I remember? Why, she would hang on him,
> As if increase of appetite had grown
> By what it fed on; and yet, within a month—
> Let me not think on't—Frailty, thy name is woman!
> A little month, or ere those shoes were old
> With which she follow'd my poor father's body,
> Like Niobe, all tears: why she, even she,—
> O God! a beast, that wants discourse of reason,
> Would have mourned longer—married with mine uncle,
> My father's brother, but no more like my father
> Than I to Hercules: within a month:
> Ere yet the salt of most unrighteous tears
> Had left the flushing in her galled eyes,
> She married. O! most wicked speed, to post

With such dexterity to incestuous sheets.
It is not nor it cannot come to good: 30
But break, my heart; for I must hold my tongue.   [I, 2]

Clearly the burden of the speech is Hamlet's disgust with life and
the most immediate cause of his disgust, his mother's marriage.
What more do the particulars of the expression tell us? Granted
that those first two lines are a straightforward desire for death.
They do not, however, insist upon an anguished desire—the reading one usually hears. In fact, the next two lines suggest a very real
qualification for all of the first four. It has always seemed to me that
irony is at the center of Hamlet's observations, by which I mean an
ability to see through his own emotions, thus often laughing at
them. That couplet at the end of the long "Seems Madam" speech
in the preceding scene has always been for me a kind of coming
away from the intensity of his emotion, whether from shame at the
outburst or a realization of the inadequacy of the explanation. At
any rate the rhyme allows him a kind of self-deprecation that seems
central to my view of his character. So too in the soliloquy I am
never comfortable with the reading of "Everlasting" with absolute
reverence. There is something a little overstated in calling God "the
Everlasting" which has always given the line a laugh almost of
derision, so that the "O God! God!" is at first an appeal and then
a rather derisive denial. Certainly his need for God, for some
absolute answer, some unquestioned truth, is real, but nothing in
his experience says that it is a need that must be fulfilled. It is this
unsureness that really underlies the despair in the speech. How
much he wants to give up! " 'tis an unweeded garden"—let it go.
And yet, despite this, there is that insistent plea for an answer in
"That it should come to this!" What brought up Claudius? Is it
Hamlet's rather witty mind again that sees Claudius as one of those
"things rank and gross in nature [that] / Possess it merely"? Or is it
the throne that he refers to here? At any rate, there he is, the
reminder of that other king, "So excellent a king," who not yet two
months dead is still forgotten by this court of armbands.
    And perhaps the second throne, the queen's, reminds him of his
mother. At any rate, something here reminds him of the most
infuriating and painful fact to which he must now accustom himself, namely his mother's, the queen's, marriage. It takes him nine
lines, continually interrupted by emotion that won't let him com-

SUBTEXTS IN SHAKESPEARE   51

plete the thought, to say that his mother is "married with [his] uncle." And though I think the emphasis can be as much on the horror of the man who has taken his father's place as on the fact that his mother has remarried, it is certainly these nine lines, and in fact the repetition in the following four, that incline some interpreters to the incest theme. The intensity of his concern, the need to convince the world of his right to fury, the uncontrolled interruptions ("Heaven and earth! / Must I remember?" and "Let me not think on't") have so overwhelmed him that even his self-disgust disappears in his indignation at her action. The repetition "within a month," "A little month," the broken phrases which build the explanation for some ten lines without a conclusion, certainly force the actor into an open plea for justification.

Here, it seems to me, the most important problem for the actor is not to create a character, is not appearance—the costumer's suit of mourning will take care of that—but to persuade us of the validity of his conviction that his feelings are justified. The soliloquy is a poem; the actor is the speaker of that poem, and his most important instruments of persuasion are the words. Unlike Yeats, who insisted that Shakespeare at his best forgot character and moved to pure poetry, I would say that all great Shakespearean poetry is very precise delineation of character—so precise, in fact, that the best means of realizing it is by fully understanding its verbal force and the human motivation for saying it. This is, after all, what acting is. It sounds so simple and yet it is so difficult, difficult because it means that the great Shakespearean actor must not only understand and respond to the most sophisticated of verbal structures, the poem, but also be able to know why he uses that particular structure to persuade his audience or his fellow actors. He must know, further, the difference in that collection of words between the real emotion of, say, Hamlet at Ophelia's grave, and the conventionally correct emotion of Laertes. He must be able to hear in his own ear the difference between

> O! treble woe
> Fall ten times treble on that cursed head,
> Whose wicked deed thy most ingenious sense
> Depriv'd thee of! [V, 1]

and

> I lov'd Ophelia: forty thousand brothers
> Could not, with all their quantity of love
> Make up my sum.   [V, 1]

After all, Hamlet does:

> What is he whose grief
> Bears such an emphasis? whose phrase of sorrow
> Conjures the wandering stars, and makes them stand
> Like wonder-wounded hearers? this is I,
> Hamlet the Dane.   [V, 1]

His ear must be as discerning as a critic's in hearing the precise intention of the poet, since if it's good poetry, the intention is spelled out as exactly as in a lyric poem. Tone of voice, one of the tools in a lyricist's writing, becomes the whole focus of the actor's interpretation.

I might point out in passing that such an analysis of lyric poetry is, for me, the best way of understanding it. I am not speaking here of such obvious examples of the dramatic monologue as Browning develops or even such direct addresses as Donne's "The Canonization," but *all* lyric poetry. The poet is, after all, addressing somebody or something, whether it is a friend, the west wind, his own conscience, a material-minded reader (I think of Frost's "Provide, Provide") or a hopefuly sympathetic world at large. He is, after all, a speaker just as an actor is, and I suspect generally that that speaker is no more the poet than Shakespeare is Macbeth. In both cases there is a voice defined by the way language is put together, a voice we can identify. If we are critics, we define it and evaluate it against our experiences as human beings. If we are actors or readers, we define it, let it work on us, and then recreate it out of our experience as human beings. An actor, like a musical performer, is not always conscious of that definition process, but he, like a musician, must be able to read the score, understand its notation, and find ways to make sense out of its transitions. He must, in other words, know how to read—and poetry is not only as precise, but is often as unique a vocabulary as musical notation.

As I have suggested in my comparison of Shakespeare with Miller and Williams, language, one tool in a dramatist's vocabulary, is not always used with equal precision.[3] When it is used with care, as in Shakespeare's plays, it clearly must be attended to with the same care one accords to lyric poems. The technique that creates the tone of voice in both forms is the same, though clearly the context in which the poems work is different. It is this recognition that makes one respect Redgrave's suspicions about Stanislavsky's limitations. Certainly the ability to read poetry, to understand a Shakespearean soliloquy in the same way one understands a Shakespearean sonnet or a lyric by Dylan Thomas, is essential equipment for the actor of Shakespeare. It is not, however, the only necessary equipment. Indeed, if all drama were soliloquy, we could simply examine the poem-speech and give it correctly.

Unfortunately, drama like human discourse is a public affair. This is not to say that careful examination is not necessary in dialogue. It is just as necessary as in the soliloquy, but there are in dialogue other considerations to attend to as well. It is here that more than poetic concern is necessary. It is possible in a soliloquy to be fairly naked in one's expression because no one is around to keep the face before. But in most dramatic speech there is such a someone around, either to overhear or, more often, to be talked to. In public we do not express our naked souls; it is both embarrassing and, what is worse, unhelpful to the point of our discourse. If one wants something from someone else—and that is, it seems to me, the reason for most conversation (whether it be a favor, an admission, an agreement, or simply attention) —one does not bare his soul and expect pity or understanding to move his hearer to grant the favor he is asking. The favor may well be in his head, but the conversation may be about all kinds of other matters. And this is as true in plays as in life.

It is this underlying intention, sometimes sure, sometimes vague, that I call *subtext*. It is this unspoken intention in the character that must be realized by the actor; that is, he must have some reason for being on stage besides spouting pretty language. Or perhaps it would be more precise to say that the pretty poetry he recites is only the externalization of why he is on stage. The underlying intention

---

[3] I think it only fair to add that modern playwrights have certain tools in their theatrical vocabulary that Shakespeare did not. Setting and lighting, to name but two obvious ones, were hardly artist's tools in a theatre that used the same setting for all plays and performed under whatever light nature gave.

that motivates what he says is his real reason for being there; if he has none, he had better leave. Without it, an audience is listening to a public speaker or lecturer, not an actor in a play. Today at least, it is this intention that most interests an audience, and one of the actor's main jobs is to let us know what that intention is. I do not mean to suggest a single, simple-minded intention that is brought on stage for a scene and never changes until the scene ends. Clearly it changes continually according to what the character hears, what he himself says, and what he does or what is done to him. The important point is that the need for such a motivation to what he says is as important in classic drama as it is in modern.[4]

Basically my term *intention* here is, as I understand it, Stanislavsky's subtext translated into, hopefully, concrete detail. My own interpretation of subtext owes much to John Russell Brown in his two articles on subtext.[5] I propose, however, to go somewhat further in how subtext can be used. Brown's concern is primarily the character's inner life as it can be deduced by the text, by Shakespeare's way of phrasing. This concern is certainly valid; it is, I think, a technique that actors must use, whether consciously or not, in order to understand the transitions in any given speech. But to carry this concern further, what I am interested in is the actor's intention, his real purpose in being on stage, regardless of the one he may state. It is the action he wishes to perform that concerns us, not simply the kind of person he is. In fact, the kind of person he is may be largely determined by the casting, not by one's acting ability. If I am five-foot-six and cast as Othello, no amount of stretching or tiptoeing is going to make me a six-foot commanding general. The best Othello my five-foot-six can give is the one that comes from my way of doing what Othello must do in the course of the play. I do not imitate a "character"—I wish we could burn that word out of all discussions of dramatic production—I must, as an actor, simply recreate in my body the attitude Shakespeare has created, and that attitude is defined by the things I must do or not do, in the course of the play. What Shakespeare has given the actor is the words that tell him how to do what he must do. His job is to

---

4 Robert Lewis, in his very sensible book, *Method or Madness* (Heinemann, 1960), explains my sense of intention very precisely on pages 30–31.
5 "Shakespeare's Subtext I" and "Shakespeare's Subtext II," *Tulane Drama Review* (Fall and Winter 1963, respectively).

find the event, the activity, that makes sense out of those words, to discover what he is on stage to accomplish, given Shakespeare's words as the manner of doing it.

Such a concern may sound obvious, one that an actor takes for granted. Often he does and can. If, after all, in *The Taming of the Shrew*, Petruchio announces to the audience before his first meeting with Kate that he will "attend her here, / And woo her with some spirit when she comes" and then goes on to tell us how he will do it, we can be pretty certain that he is aware of what he is on stage for. So, too, Richard III announces to us his intention to woo Anne, Hamlet to berate his mother, Lear to divide his kingdom, and so on. Certainly there is no difficulty finding the action each must accomplish in these cases, but I think that even here actors need to be *reminded* of the action, the thing they are to do. Even when the intention is clearly stated, there is often a tendency for an actor or a director to forget it and to play the words—to show off to an audience rather than to *woo* Anne, to look for funny business with Kate rather than to *woo* her. Shakespeare's language is seductive, and the British concern in the past with poetry for its own sake and the resultant kinds of performances have done much to establish a way of doing his plays that allows an actor to forget his intentions altogether. Certainly if Hamlet remembers not only his intention to "speak daggers not use them" with his mother but also the difficulty he might have in remembering that intention, one might well see a real struggle in him to keep himself from losing his temper with her. I don't think I have ever seen a Hamlet in the closet scene who was seriously worried about keeping the soul of Nero out of his bosom. I have seen him angry with his mother; I have not seen his attempt, however unsuccessful, to be reasonable with her. In other words, his intention, which is at least partly to control himself, is not fully realized or attended to.

Now, such a statement may overlook what happens to intention once it comes on stage. In other words, no matter what Hamlet may intend to do when he arrives, those intentions are sharply qualified by what he encounters after he arrives. It is precisely this qualification and how it comes about that is dramatic. If Hamlet arrived determined on what he was to do and then did it with no attention or apparent need to deal with what his mother said or did, we would have a speech or series of speeches, not a scene. Clearly in this scene whatever he comes on to do is sharply qualified by the very appearance of his mother. I would like to quote a bit of it and examine intention:

HAMLET [*within*]   Mother, mother, mother!
QUEEN   I'll warrant you;
     Fear me not: withdraw. I hear him coming.

[*Enter* HAMLET.]

HAMLET   Now, mother, what's the matter?
QUEEN   Hamlet, thou has thy father much offended.
HAMLET   Mother, you have my father much offended.
QUEEN   Come, come, you answer with an idle tongue.
HAMLET   Go, go, you question with a wicked tongue.
QUEEN   Why, how now, Hamlet!
HAMLET   What's the matter now?
QUEEN   Have you forgot me?
HAMLET   No, by the rood, not so:
     You are the queen, your husband's brother's wife;
     And,—would it were not so!—you are my mother.
QUEEN   Nay then, I'll set those to you that can speak.
HAMLET   Come, come, and sit you down; you shall not budge;
     You go not, til I set you up a glass
     Where you may see the inmost part of you.   [III, 4]

I quote but this much to demonstrate how quickly intentions may change and what a multitude of them may be at play underneath the text. Hamlet's first three "Mother's" hardly sound like the man under control who would speak daggers but use none. But then, we must remember that between Hamlet's statement of intention and his present arrival on stage, he has seen Claudius at prayer, almost killed him, stayed his hand, and rushed to his mother's chambers. That experience with Claudius might well have changed his emotional and even intellectual desires. He is excited as we first hear him, and one suspects it is that excitement he will bring on stage. It is not until his first speech that we hear a calmer Hamlet and the first question we must ask is, "Why? What changed him?"

I think it is simply his mother's presence, the fact of facing her, and in facing her the remembrance of what he came to do. He remembers first that it is she who has called him, that he would like to convince her that he has come quietly at her bidding, not simply because of his own need to accuse. I do not mean to suggest that he manages control either easily or convincingly. He is a highly wrought-up young man—so wrought-up that the queen fears for her life very shortly after his arrival. But the very fact that he can remember and act on this memory (considering the excitement of "Mother, mother, mother!") suggests, I think, his attempt at rational discourse. What happens is that her first words bring up the very subject he must confront her with, and though he tries to control himself—I think the grammatical parallelism of his answer suggests control rather than passion—the very way he twists her reference to Claudius to his concern with his father shows he is on the attack, not simply a son listening to his mother. The attack continues in his next speech, which is a little less controlled. At least in my own reading, the repetition "Go, go" makes the line sharper, quicker. But note his next response, "What's the matter, now?" Certainly, this suggests a return to even temper.

The struggle between attack and rational discourse is still going on. It goes on until the stabbing of Polonius, an act that releases much of the passion biting at Hamlet and allows him to talk straight or at least openly about what most concerns him: "[to] kill a king and marry with his brother." The excitement of the near murder of Claudius, coupled with the need to control himself, pushes Hamlet into the strange behavior that both the queen and the audience might well call mad. An actor needs to know precisely what is pushing him; he cannot simply play madness, or even something apparently more actable, hysteria. He needs concrete details, an intention modified by the text, indeed given finally by the text, but perhaps only suggested in the words of the text themselves. Hamlet brings with him what has most immediately happened to him and a desire to do something about it. The resultant drama is how this intention, with whatever emotional coloring surrounds it, is manifested on stage by what happens there.

It is for this reason that an actor must know what he wants to do on stage and also what has happened to him before he gets there. It is not that he consciously uses these motivations or intentions, but he does let them work on him, much as a painter lets his environment work on him. A painter friend of mine whose latest studio happens to have a stage at one end finds himself working on both space relations and the meanings of settings because the stage is there. Chances are he would not have been interested if it weren't there. This is not to say he is interested in stages and consciously painting them; it is to say that his environment is part of what he paints. For the actor, his emotional environment and what he wants to accomplish are the material out of which he creates. The differences in the method of accomplishment are primarily the differences in the personality of the creator. To a lesser extent but as important to the final outcome are the environment and intentions the actor chooses. My point is that no actor who moves us operates without such intentions and environment. As directors, we cannot tell an actor how to play a scene—that was taken care of, for better or worse, when he was cast—but we can help create for him the environment and the intentions out of which we think he should work. It is the limiting of such intentions and the modification of such environment that are probably the best way of touching the emotional commitments of the actor.

I have suggested that intentions are available for any scene. I think that is correct, even something as apparently unmotivated as Ophelia's madness. Ophelia is usually played as being distraught and totally unintelligible. This seems to me wrong, to destroy the chaotic kind of sense she makes. The key, I think, is the gentleman's speech to the queen just preceding Ophelia's first mad entrance. He urges the queen to see the girl because, he says:

> She speaks much of her father; says she hears
> There's tricks i' the world; and hems, and beats her heart;
> Spurns enviously at straws; speaks things in doubt,
> That carry but half sense; her speech is nothing.
> Yet the unshaped use of it doth move
> The hearers to collection; they yawn at it,
> And botch the words up fit to their own thoughts;
> Which, as her winks, and nods, and gestures yield them,
> Indeed would make one think there might be thought,
> Though nothing sure, yet much unhappily. [IV, 5]

People "botch the words up fit to their own thoughts," a situation not unlike a good deal of the play, though here much more apparent. People, everyone but Claudius, for example, have misread Hamlet. Communication is always difficult, and words make strange impressions. And strange perhaps, but definite, I think, are the impressions Ophelia's words make on the king and queen. Let me quote the first mad scene and suggest a possible reading:

[*Reenter* HORATIO, *with* OPHELIA.]

OPHELIA   Where is the beauteous majesty of Denmark?

QUEEN   How now, Ophelia!
OPHELIA [*sings*]   How should I your true love know
                    From another one?
                    By his cockle hat and staff,
                    And his sandal shoon.
QUEEN   Alas, sweet lady, what imports this song?
OPHELIA Say you? nay, pray you, mark.
    [*sings*] He is dead and gone, lady,
                    He is dead and gone;
                    At his head a grass-green turf,
                    At his heels a stone.
QUEEN   Nay, but Ophelia,—
OPHELIA Pray you, mark
    [*sings*] White his shroud as the mountain snow,—

[*Enter* KING.]

QUEEN   Alas, look here, my lord.
OPHELIA [*sings*]   Larded all with flowers;
                    Which bewept to the grave did not go
                    With true-love showers.
KING   How do you, pretty lady?
OPHELIA Well, God 'ild you! They say the owl was a baker's daughter.
    Lord, we know what we are, but know not what we may be. God be at
    your table!
KING   Conceit upon her father.
OPHELIA Pray you, let's have no words of this; but when they ask you
    what it means, say you this:
    [*sings*] To-morrow is Saint Valentine's day,
                    All in the morning betime,
                    And I a maid at your window,
                    To be your Valentine.
                    Then up he rose, and donn'd his clothes,
                    And dupp'd the chamber-door;
                    Let in the maid that out a maid
                    Never departed more.
KING   Pretty Ophelia!
OPHELIA Indeed, la, without an oath, I'll make an end on't:
    [*sings*] By Gis and by Saint Charity,
                    Alack, and fie for shame!
                    Young men will do't, if they come to't;
                    By cock, they are to blame.
                    Quoth she, before you tumbled me,
                    You promised me to wed.
                    So would I ha' done, by yonder sun,
                    An thou hadst not come to my bed.
KING   How long hath she been thus?

CHAPTER III

OPHELIA I hope all will be well. We must be patient: but I cannot choose but weep, to think they should lay him i' the cold ground. My brother shall know of it: and so I thank you for your good counsel. Come, my coach! Good night, ladies; good night, sweet ladies; good night, good night. [*Exit.*] [IV, 5]

Too often this scene is played with a general air of distraction, as if Ophelia recognized no one or sensed no difference among the people who come onto the stage. And yet her tone changes and seems directed to whom she speaks. It is not accidental, I think, that her opening speech to the queen is about who her true love is. It is not as if she came on to tell the queen this, but seeing her and overwhelmed with her own sense of death (of her father) and love (lust?) (for Hamlet), it is understandable why she says it, or rather how she says it. She pauses as if to be sure of whom she is looking at, and then suddenly what she recognizes is that woman who has had two husbands. The pilgrim reference in the last two lines of the first verse, which (as many editors remark) is a common disguise for lovers, might well make the whole song, at least to the queen's ears, an open attack on her adultery and second marriage. What did the gentleman say?—"And botch the words up fit to their own thoughts." The justification on Ophelia's part may be only the remembrance of Gertrude's two men; it may also be some sense of something she doesn't like in Claudius. Her second verse, calling the queen's attention back to her (I assume if the queen feels the attack, she has turned to get away from it), might be a reference to old Hamlet, as if Ophelia were answering the queen's question as to who had died. It might also be to her own father. Chances are it starts as Hamlet's father, and the very thoughts of death turn the reference more immediately to Polonius. One certainly senses that the last verse is too personal a remembrance for Hamlet's father and is a reenactment of the more recent funeral.

The remembrance, however, is cut short by a new voice, a voice she doesn't like, a voice to which she answers as a crude slut. Why? If particular motivation is needed, say that she saw something in the king's manner at the play scene, his breakdown, that made her recognize his evil. But what is important is that it is the king's voice that changes her manner, and it should be clear that it is the king's voice that she has heard. She might turn to verify it—yes, she might point, he is the one. Certainly the "we know what we are, but know not what we may be" is as applicable to Claudius as to her father. Again I think he should react as if he felt it. His response is certainly not very strong and could well look little more than a cover for his own momentary confusion. It is also interesting that her bawdy little song is addressed to the king. Something in him suggests his lechery, seems to call forth an attack from her. Her "without an oath, I'll make an end on't" is certainly some kind of attack since the last verse opens with two oaths. Toward the end of that verse, however, her thoughts turn again to Hamlet and the confusion of their affair, an affair called lust by her father, love by Hamlet, then lust by Hamlet. What was it about? In some ways the "before you tumbled me" is almost a wish. It is a virgin's desire to know about sex, not a trollop's admission of it. At any rate, it turns her from the king long enough for him to speak to Gertrude before Ophelia's final speech, the beginning of which is perhaps the closest to sanity.

There is perhaps more unmotivated distraction in her second entrance. Laertes' "This nothing's more than matter" suggests that the important thing in her singing here is the broken picture she presents—broken, we shouldn't forget, by the same deceit and hypocrisy that Hamlet has so fruitlessly but movingly attempted to combat. Nevertheless, the rue, the fennel, the columbine, and their presentation can again do much to show her feelings about the king and queen, and their reactions can show something of the impression the attack makes. It is not only ironic, but part of the tragic point that Ophelia can only understand the king and queen, can only get through to them, in her madness. She has no more success in the everyday social world than Hamlet does. The parallels between the two are not accidental, and a clear conception by Ophelia of whom she speaks to and what that speaking means makes those parallels clear.

I have talked here about Ophelia's intention as it changes and is shaped on stage, not of what it was as she entered. Frankly, I don't know that I could guess at much more than confusion, at an attempt to sort out her questions about Hamlet, her father, the king, and the queen. The point is that, once she sees or hears the queen or king, a new sense of direction, almost a sense of recognition, takes place that focuses what Ophelia is doing.

If this illustration suggests what intention is, it does not provide any of the ways to accomplish it. Often, no problems in explicating intention arise. One clarifies what he or she wants to do and then comes on stage to do it, letting himself be moved by what occurs in the process of this attempt. Many times, however, the spelling out of intention is not enough. I remember working with a Desdemona on the following scene:

EMILIA   How goes it now? He looks gentler than he did.
DESDEMONA   He says he will return incontinent;
   He hath commanded me to go to bed,
   And bade me to dismiss you.
EMILIA   Dismiss me!
DESDEMONA   It was his bidding; therefore, good Emilia,
   Give me my nightly wearing, and adieu:
   We must not now displease him.
EMILIA   I would you had never seen him!
DESDEMONA   So would not I; my love doth so approve him,
   That even his stubbornness, his checks and frowns,—
   Prithee, unpin me,—have grace and favour in them.
EMILIA   I have laid those sheets you bade me on the bed.
DESDEMONA   All's one. Good faith, how foolish are our minds!
   If I do die before thee, prithee, shroud me
   In one of those same sheets.
EMILIA   Come, come, you talk.
DESDEMONA   My mother had a maid call'd Barbara:
   She was in love, and he she lov'd prov'd mad
   And did forsake her; she had a song of 'willow';
   An old thing 'twas, but it express'd her fortune,
   And she died singing it: that song to-night
   Will not go from my mind; I have much to do,
   But to go hang my head all at one side,
   And sing like poor Barbara. Prithee, dispatch.
EMILIA   Shall I go fetch your night-gown?
DESDEMONA   No, unpin me here.
   This Lodovico is a proper man.
EMILIA   A very handsome man.
DESDEMONA   He speaks well.
EMILIA   I know a lady in Venice would have walked barefoot to Palestine
   for a touch of his nether lip.
DESDEMONA
   [singing] The poor soul sat sighing by a sycamore tree,
            Sing all a green willow;

Her hand on her bosom, her head on her knee,
    Sing willow, willow, willow:
The fresh streams ran by her, and murmur'd her moans;
    Sing willow, willow, willow;
Her salt tears fell from her, and soften'd the stones;—

Lay by these:

[*singing*] Sing willow, willow, willow;

Prithee, hie thee; he'll come anon:

[*singing*] Sing all a green willow must be my garland.
        Let nobody blame him, his scorn I approve,—
Nay, that's not next.—Hark! who is't that knocks?
EMILIA It's the wind.
DESDEMONA
[*singing*] I call'd my love false love; but what said he then?
        Sing willow, willow, willow:
        If I court moe women, you'll couch with moe men."
So, get thee gone; good night. [IV, 3]

The changes in Desdemona's intentions, or changes in interest, seem to me fairly easy to determine. She has returned from Othello and, up to "So would not I," her concern is to prepare for bed and dismiss Emilia. That direction is momentarily changed by Emilia's "I would you had never seen him," and her next speech is a quick but real defense of Othello. Again at "All's one," she returns to undressing and more specifically to her remembrance of the willow song and what it reminds her of. From here to the end of the scene as I have quoted it her concern is that song. There are four interruptions: her first injunction to Emilia, "Prithee, dispatch"; then "Lay by these"; and rather quickly, "Prithee hie thee; he'll come anon"; and finally, "Hark! who is't that knocks?" Her major concern, once she gets to it, is the willow song and what it recalls to her. Her first problem in the scene, however, is getting to that song. Why does she think of it? What preceded it in the scene? What brings the song, with all its implications, to her?

Perhaps the first thing to recognize is what does *not* get her there. Certainly a casual, or even not so casual, conversation with Emilia is no particular help. She has not come to the bedroom to talk; she has been sent there by Othello after being slapped and called a whore. Surely part of what is on her mind is this treatment; at least, such a concern is most apt to be on the mind of the actress who is trying to recreate the situation Shakespeare gives us. Such a subtext is certainly hinted at some twenty lines into the scene in her "Good faith, how foolish are our minds! / If I do die before thee, prithee, shroud me / In one of those same sheets." The actress is asked to consider other possibilities than making conversation with Emilia. I think it is further suggested that her mind is specifically on Othello in the sharpness of her "So would not I" in her response to Emilia's "I would you had never seen him." Even if she cannot or does not choose to speak of Othello, he is with her. She may push the immediacy of him away in "All's one," but her concern with death, which immediately follows (with the end of *her* life, one suspects), is a reflection cast up from her feelings about Othello and his recent treatment of her. I do not mean to suggest a morbid dwelling on the subject—indeed, her reference to Lodovico is evidence of her desire to think elsewhere—but the song and its implications keep coming back to her. She can't avoid them. Her love for Othello and her forebodings of death stemming from his treatment of her seem to be inherent in the scene, but the problem of realizing this dichotomy is not a simple one.

It seems to me that in trying to realize this subtext, this reason for saying the words Shakespeare gives us, improvisations can be very helpful. I would think in this case not only improvisations about outside situations or with other people—a Lodovico-Desdemona scene to find out what they know of each other might help an actress find a way to bring Lodovico to mind—but also what one might call a prosification would help, simply asking the actress to do this scene in her own words, filling in all the thoughts which are underneath what she says. The hope here is that, by using her own words, she might discover for herself and for her director both problems in transitions and underlying emotional connotations that Shakespeare's language had not called up but that her own language might, feelings that the lines of Shakespeare in their poetic formality may not have immediately created.

The following is a paraphrase of such an improvisation. I do not remember all of the things that happened, but the first time through sounded like this:

EMILIA Are things better? He doesn't look so angry.
DESDEMONA He said he is coming to bed right away, and bid me to dismiss you.

EMILIA What!

DESDEMONA That's what he bid me; therefore, give me my nightgown and leave me.

EMILIA I wish you had never seen him.

DESDEMONA Oh, I don't.

At this point I stopped the two because nothing was happening except a paraphrase of the text. None of the motivation underneath that text appeared. This in itself proved a good deal. It was clear that no subtext existed for the two—none whatever. The two actresses at this stage in their work were aware only of the lines themselves; the reasons for speaking them were nowhere apparent. We talked again about what had happened to Desdemona before this scene, of where she had just come from, and of what her feelings were about Othello.

The second paraphrase showed us a little more:

EMILIA My dear, you look worried. Don't be. I—I'm sure he is, has changed.

DESDEMONA Yes, of course.—Yes. He is coming, Emilia, and, and, has asked me to dismiss you. I am to go to bed.

EMILIA Dismiss? Why, my dear? Why?

DESDEMONA Oh, Emilia, I don't know. I don't.—But he did. Come, help me to prepare.

EMILIA Prepare?

DESDEMONA For bed, my dear. For bed.

EMILIA I hate him.

DESDEMONA What?

EMILIA I—I wish you had never seen him.

DESDEMONA No, Emilia. No, no. [*Stops.*]

Now a number of things came clear out of this exchange. First of all, the connection between the two women, their care for each other, appeared. Second, Emilia's dislike of the man came out—that "Prepare?" with its sacrificial overtones was something Emilia did not recognize was in her before she said it. And perhaps most important was the first real hangup in transitions that Desdemona had. Given her feeling now for Emilia and her own confusions about what was to come, she had trouble saying she really loved him. Clearly, there was something more than an easy admission of her feeling, at least for this Desdemona, and gradually by working back to the text, through such paraphrasing, she found that what was really slowing her up was a way to persuade Emilia, worldly sophisticate that she is, of how, despite her worries, she did love this man.

I am obviously formulating things that the actress never verbalized. At the same time the changes in her whole behavior, operating as she began to, not as a speaker of lines, but as a human being going through a real experience of which the lines were only the verbal expression, were real. True, the move from improvisation or paraphrase back to the text is a slow one. No paraphrase, after all, is going to be the exact text that must finally be presented, and the casting out of things that don't help, the keeping of things that do, is a slow process. The joy an actor feels when he does his own scene and sees all the possibilities is often terribly misleading. He feels the paraphrase and assumes that all of it will fit into the text. Often, much of what happens is unusable, and his first response as he returns to the text is, "What good is it?" What he has discovered, however, are feelings he had not even realized existed, and many of them turn out to be usable. In other words, subtext—the things not said—are often the real reason for what is said. After all, what is rehearsal for?

This kind of work is of particular importance in the classics, in the plays that move us in a general way but do not open to us in a particular way in the same fashion that modern plays do. Albee seems much closer to our immediate lives than Shakespeare or Euripides. But if Shakespeare or Euripides is to be as real to us as Albee (hopefully, from my own view, more real), then we must know what is underneath that language as surely as we know what is underneath Albee or Chekhov. It is not an unusual procedure to rehearse Chekhov in the way I have outlined here. Why not Shakespeare? Or, for that matter, Euripides?

In a recent rehearsal for a production of *The Trojan Women,* the actress playing Hecuba had great difficulty in finding out in her first speech why she changed from the defeat of the opening of the speech to the sense of fight that characterized the end of the speech. Here is the speech in Richmond Lattimore's translation:[6]

> Rise, stricken head from the dust;
> lift up the throat. This is Troy, but Troy

6 David Grene and Richmond Lattimore, eds., *The Complete Greek Tragedies: Euripides III* (Washington Square Press, 1968).

and we, Troy's kings, are perished.
Stoop to the changing fortune.
Steer for the crossing and the death-god,
hold not life's prow on the course against
wave beat and accident.
Ah me,
what need I further for tears' occasion,
state perished, my sons, and my husband?
O massive pride that my fathers heaped
to magnificence, you meant nothing.
Must I be hushed: Were it better thus?
Should I cry a lament?
Unhappy, accursed,
limbs cramped, I lie
backed on earth's stiff bed.
O head, O temples
and sides; sweet, to shift,
let the tired spine rest
weight eased by the sides alternate,
against the strain of the tears' song
where the stricken people find music yet
in the song undanced of their wretchedness.

You ship prows, that the fugitive
oars swept back to blessed Ilium
over the sea's blue water
by the placid harbors of Hellas
to the flute's grim beat
and the swing of the shrill boat whistles;
you made the crossing, made fast ashore
the Egyptians skill, the sea cables,
alas, by the coasts of Troy;
it was you, ships, that carried the fatal bride
of Menelaos, Castor her brother's shame,
the stain on Eurotas.
Now she has killed
the sire of the fifty sons,
Priam; me, unhappy Hecuba,
she drove on this reef of ruin.

Such a state I keep
to sit by the tents of Agamemnon.
I am led captive from my house, an old, unhappy woman,
like my city ruined and pitiful.
Come then, sad wives of the Trojans
whose spears were bronze,
their daughters, brides of disaster,
let us mourn the smoke of Ilium.

CHAPTER III

And I, as among winged birds
the mother, lead out
the clashing cry, the song; not that song
wherein once long ago
when I held the sceptre of Priam
my feet were queens of the choir and led
the proud dance to the gods of Phrygia.

The actress had carefully paraphrased the ideas so that she was quite sure of what the transitions were and what the meaning was. The first line and a half was an attempt at dignity, an attempt to stand up despite what had happened to her, but the rest of that first verse was a recognition of the impossibility of doing it. It was a collapse. Why, after all, should she? Wasn't it easier to quit? After all, the dignity, the pride of being queen, had only cost her the excessive degradation she now experienced. Why not rest, swaying from side to side, resting against the ease of resignation?

The second verse, describing the ships, gives her nothing to change that conviction—until she comes to a remembrance of "the fatal bride of Menelaos," Helen. It is she who has brought Hecuba to this ruin, caused the death of Priam. It is she who has put Hecuba in this condition to end up as Agamemnon's slave. And now with her "Come then, sad wives of the Trojans," her attitude changes and she will fight; she will stand up and "lead out the clashing cry, the song," even though it is "not that song wherein once" she led as queen. The problem clearly is: Why the change? To paraphrase my Hecuba, she said:

The thought of Helen arouses hatred in me and motivates my rise, my reason to fight. Helen's punishment is my one hope for justice, a just revenge. Once that hope comes to me, I feel I have a duty to perform to preserve the honor and pride of all Trojans still alive. Once again I am a queen, unbeaten. I will lead "the clashing cry, the song."

Now, hate for Helen is not one of the prerequisites for Hecuba if we simply read the text. And yet this human motivation gives Hecuba a human reason for standing up. I don't imagine anyone in the audience was aware of that subtext, but they were aware of a woman with strength—no self-pity—but dignity. And that is essential for Hecuba if we are to see the almost unbelievable strength she finally has in saying, "On, on, into the slave's life." That feeling for Helen, though it is not spelled out in the text, does something else for Hecuba. It defines her in her confrontation with Helen. So angry does she become as she listens to Helen's false logic and watches her womanly seductiveness work on Menelaos that she attacks Menelaos in her defense against Helen. So angry is she at Helen that her temper pushes Menelaos toward Helen rather than away from her. Clearly, in Helen's speech she has come far toward seducing Menelaos into believing her, since the chorus says at the end of her speech at the climax of the play:

> O Queen of Troy, stand by your children and your country!
> Break down the beguilement of this woman; since she speaks
> well, and has done wickedly. This is dangerous.

And Hecuba has seen this, has seen the fall of Troy all over again in this seductive bitch's blandishments.

Again it is not important that the audience see more than Helen's success with Menelaos and Hecuba's loss of the fight. What is important is that they hear a human being, not a speech. I think that concern with subtext as well as text is necessary to discover that attitude.

IV*

Restoration and
Eighteenth-Century Comedy

Careful attention to language, to what is underneath it, and to its value for actors and directors is perhaps as vital to an understanding of producing Restoration comedy as to any body of English drama in the canon. With Sheridan I think we come to the end (at least temporarily) of this concern with language as precise definer and to the beginning of something else. In this chapter, I would like to look at pieces of four plays to show how this concern can help one produce this body of plays. In all of these comedies—in fact, I think one could say in all comedies that are usually defined as "comedies of manners"—the central concern is the wooing game. In one way or another all such plays seem to concern themselves with how men and women live together, either in wedlock, out of wedlock, or in that strange hiatic period prior to wedlock but with wedlock in mind. Because almost by definition, flirtation means posing as something one is not, at least something one is not *all the time,* the sense of game is usually understood in such plays.

Most often, the game concerns the web woman spins to catch and marry a man, and man's attempts to avoid that web and hence the marriage, but still have the woman. One thinks of Dorimant in *The Man of Mode,* of Horner in *The Country Wife,* of Archer in *The Beaux' Stratagem,* or the Surface brothers in *The School for Scan-*

* This chapter was originally published in a substantially different version as "Restoration Comedy: An Approach to Modern Production" in *Drama Survey,* Nos. I and 2 (Winter 1968–1969).

dal, to name but a few. Mirabell's case in *The Way of the World* could be classed as an exception, since he seems at least as anxious for marriage as does Millamant, just as Berenthia's interest in the already married Loveless in *The Relapse* would need some qualification. But in either case we would not cheat the plays to insist that the major concern of both *The Relapse* and *The Way of the World* is how the sexes live with each other and the kinds of games they play to make that life tolerable.

The problem in most productions of such plays is to determine first what precisely the particular game or event underlying the language is and second how it is being played. In both cases the language can tell us a good deal; in some plays it is the only sure clue we have. I am assuming not only that the games being played are still in operation (Otherwise, how would anyone understand at all?) but that close attention to the language will suggest that they are played in much the same way. I mean by this that the language, once heard clearly, is not the quaint and outmoded strutting of some bizarre peacock now happily extinct and hence to be laughed at that so many productions of seventeenth- and eighteenth-century comedy make it, but a perfectly recognizable view of our contemporary struttings, quite as human and quite as alternately ridiculous and touching. Too often, the actors play the games for the audience's benefit rather than their own, thus denying us any insight into our own lives. It is as if we were at some kind of zoo, watching the charming but admittedly unhuman gestures of a species different from ourselves.

I can understand this. In our distance from the period, in our insistence on seeing the fops as long-dead types, as caricatures, and in our inability to recognize the flirtatious games played by Millamant and Mirabell as our own, we make of the plays museum pieces. We have even concocted a *style,* a manner of moving and talking, which has nothing to do with our own sense of reality but is our way of making the periwigs and the high heels the silly things they must have been. Who, after all, except the silliest kind of poseur, would ever dress like Witwoud, or Flutter, or even Mirabell? And so, we have as astute a critic as Brooks Atkinson saying of Ritchard's Foppington in *The Relapse* of 1950, "his stylized condescension and fripperies are all vastly entertaining, which is all that anyone should expect from a comedy." That the play might be making a pertinent comment on the difficulties of constancy between the sexes, or even of its worth, apparently never occurred to Atkinson.

It seems to me that the only possibility of producing these plays successfully is to recognize that we are basically looking at a very realistic picture of the ways in which the sexes deal with the problems of living with each other. The manifestation of the "ways" is generally a series of games, sometimes self-conscious and aware, sometimes more natural and unaware, but still like games, a playing. It is obvious that these games are still in operation in our sexual concourse; what is not so obvious is to see how the games played in the seventeenth and eighteenth centuries parallel our own. Too often in these comedies the games of that bygone age become, for the actors, pretty demonstrations of the manners of the past—games put on for the audience's benefit—not at all games played for each other. Such productions forget that Millamant is not displaying herself for the world, but to capture and hold onto Mirabell. They forget that it is to him, not us, that she is playing. We are permitted to watch. She may seem more self-conscious in her flirtation than we think ourselves, but that in no way makes her less a flirt or less anxious to get Mirabell. Her manner may not seem quite ours, but that is a matter of taste or even degree, not of kind. Laura in Strindberg's *The Father* has always seemed a bit overstated to me, but I never doubt that she has a good deal of every woman in her.

If, for example, we do not see in the famous proviso scene between Mirabell and Millamant first of all the acceptance of Mirabell by Millamant, we may miss the action of the scene entirely. Unless one recognizes the scene as an engagement party, not only is much of its meaning lost, but actors may move away from the love that underlies the scene and motivate it as simple flirtation with no other connection of any kind between the principals. I think it worth noting what I understand to be the movement of the scene to suggest how this love might manifest itself. I'll quote the first half of the scene which, for me, includes Millamant's acceptance of Mirabell and her only meaningful injunction to him:

MIRABELL [*enters*] "Like Daphne she, as lovely and as coy."
Do you lock yourself up from me, to make my search more curious? or

is this pretty artifice contrived to signify here the chase must end, and my pursuit be crowned? For you can fly no further.

MILLAMANT Vanity! no—I'll fly, and be followed to the last moment. Though I am upon the very verge of matrimony, I expect you should solicit me as much as if I were wavering at the grate of a monastery, with one foot over the threshold. I'll be solicited to the very last, nay, and afterwards.

MIRABELL What, after the last?

MILLAMANT Oh, I should think I was poor and had nothing to bestow, if I were reduced to an inglorious ease, and freed from the agreeable fatigues of solicitation.

MIRABELL But do not you know, that when favors are conferred upon instant and tedious solicitation, that they diminish in their value, and that both the giver loses the grace, and the receiver lessens his pleasure?

MILLAMANT It may be in things of common application; but never sure in love. Oh, I hate a lover that can dare to think he draws a moment's air, independent of the bounty of his mistress. There is not so impudent a thing in nature, as the saucy look of an assured man, confident of success. The pedantic arrogance of a very husband has not so pragmatical an air. Ah! I'll never marry, unless I am first made sure of my will and pleasure.

MIRABELL Would you have 'em both before marriage? Or will you be contented with the first now, and stay for the other till after grace?

MILLAMANT Ah! don't be impertinent.—My dear liberty, shall I leave thee? My faithful solitude, my darling contemplation, must I bid you then adieu? Ay-h, adieu,—my morning thoughts, agreeable wakings, indolent slumbers, all ye *douceurs*, ye *sommeils du matin*, adieu?—I can't do't, 'tis more than impossible. Positively, Mirabell, I'll lie abed in a morning as long as I please.

MIRABELL Then I'll get up in a morning as early as I please.

MILLAMANT Ah! Idle creature, get up when you wil.—And d'ye hear, I won't be called names after I'm married; positively I won't be called names.

MIRABELL Names!

MILLAMANT Ay, as wife, spouse, my dear, joy, jewel, love, sweetheart, and the rest of that nauseous cant, in which men and their wives are so fulsomely familiar—I shall never bear that—good Mirabell, don't let us be familiar or fond, nor kiss before folks, like my Lady Fadler and Sir Francis: nor go to Hyde Park together the first Sunday in a new chariot, to provoke eyes and whispers; and then never to be seen there together again; as if we were proud of one another the first week, and ashamed of one another for ever after. Let us never visit together, nor go to a play together; but let us be very strange and well bred: let us be as strange as if we had been married a great while; and as well bred as if we were not married at all.

MIRABELL   Have you any more conditions to offer? Hitherto your demands are pretty reasonable.

MILLAMANT   Trifles,—   [IV, 1]

Usually this sequence and even the scenes following are played as a most artificial courting dance with no physical contact and little if any human intercourse. And this is understandable. It would certainly appear from the language that Millamant is pushing Mirabell off, forcing him to keep his distance. She will, so she says, "fly and be followed to the last moment"—"nay, and afterwards"; she states, "Oh, I hate a lover that can dare to think he draws a moment's air, independent of the bounty of his mistress" and "I can't do't, 'tis more than impossible." Certainly the tone suggests a cool and disinterested dismissal of her suitor. And yet two things are given which cannot be ignored. First of all, the two love each other, they say so. Somehow whether they say it to each other or not, that fact is a given truth. Even Millamant will say finally to Mrs. Fainall, "Well, if Mirabell should not make a good husband, I am a lost thing;—for I find I love him violently." And though this truth is often commented on in discussions of Millamant, it is seldom if ever really played. If a woman loves a man and chastises him for taking her for granted, why shouldn't that love appear, even nakedly? This scene usually shows us a Millamant running from Mirabell—or circling him. Given that she loves him and halfway through the above quotation is going to admit it by accepting him—for certainly that is what she does in the line "Positively, Mirabell, I'll lie abed in a morning as long as I please"—why can't she be pursuing him, pleading with him, however lightly, to keep pursuing her, keep desiring her, even after their marriage?

If one were to paraphrase the exchange in modern, unbrilliant witticism, she would be saying something like:

Look, just because we are going to get married, I hope you don't think you can take me for granted. I mean, you do recognize that my love, my desire to live with you rests, at least in part, on the belief that you will not take me for granted, but recognize me always as the person you are wooing—not as a thing called a wife.

Clearly, such a plea cannot be made baldly. Who would hear it as other than a silly injunction to be dismissed as all aphorisms are dismissed? It must be phrased lightly, originally, and charmingly, so that it can be recognized as a personal truth not a general one. But that does not mean it is not given with all the directness and physical appeal that might convince the man one loves that he will enjoy, rather than be burdened with, such a wife. My Millamant will appeal to Mirabell, touch him, want him, love him—not run from him. Where did the assumption come from that Restoration heroes and heroines never touch each other? Is it from all those "Nay, good sir, I hope you do not think" kinds of lines that persuade producers of Restoration comedy that life was a continuous hands-off policy until bedtime? Perhaps. Though it seems to me that such lines might just as easily suggest precisely the opposite, namely, that hands were all too often where they should not be.

I think that the first recognition that actors must have of this scene is that it is an engagement party, and I think rehearsals would much benefit if the actors played it, to begin with, in front of the fire on a winter's evening or under a summer moon. Until they discover the human fact of physical connection in the scene—a given, after all, to any full-blooded connection between man and woman—the scene will remain an *artificial* game, not the more unconscious but essentially *real* game of love, a game that culminates in Millamant's acceptance of Mirabell, in that most unlikely line about lying abed in a morning, a line that demands some human and affectionate response of joy from Mirabell before his lightly given joke. For while it is true that one does not spend time talking the thing to pieces in this world, actors and finally audiences must recognize that love and marriage and a recognition of their joy are in the scene. Millamant tries to follow Mirabell's lead and stay light with her "Idle creature, get up when you wil.—And d'ye hear, I won't be called names after I'm married; positively I won't be called names," but she doesn't stay light. I would have her take some time and work for a very real shift to seriousness in her speech beginning "good Mirabell, don't let us be familiar," a seriousness that Mirabell hears and visually responds to before his gentle reminder to come away from talking too much about it, in "Have you any more conditions to offer? Hitherto your demands are pretty reasonable."

At this point, Millamant takes the hint, and the rest of the scene is a sharing of what to both of them are obviously silly conditions or, to put it more precisely, serious conditions about mutual respect for each other's independence, a mutual recognition of what for them constitutes good taste, and a clear understanding that marriage leads to children and a household and is not simply an extended love affair. The conditions are expressed with a lightness that makes it clear Mirabell and Millamant do not need to seriously examine the issue. In seeing the same world, they can laugh at the conditions they give each other for living in it, because they recognize their own agreement almost before the conditions are voiced. I think the scene runs a little like most postengagement discussions, lightly and jocularly. "Oh, at least twenty-two children" and "We won't let mother in the house until we're sure we can lock her in the guest bedroom" and "We will see only Bogart movies on every third Thursday." It is their sense of humor, their refusal to let the evening be spent only in body-clutching that makes them such charming adults.

I don't mean to suggest by the last sentence that the body is not an essential and recognized part of their relationship. I can't help but believe that at the end of her "My dear liberty, shall I leave thee?" speech, Millamant's "Positively, Mirabell, I'll lie abed in a morning as long as I please" is a body-stretching invitation, an offer of the delights of her body, just as Mirabell's response, "Then I'll get up in a morning as early as I please," delivered after however great a pause of interest, is a jocular refusal, an attempt at one-upmanship to keep himself his own man without at all denying his interest in her as a woman. Certainly the last smiling cut, strangely enough also her acceptance of him, is her "Ah! Idle creature, get up when you wil." It is, in fact, to be returned to later when Mirabell states his conditions for her behavior during pregnancy:

MIRABELL . . . . when you shall be breeding—
MILLAMANT Ah! name it not.
MIRABELL Which may be presumed, with a blessing on our endeavors—.
MILLAMANT Odious endeavors! [IV, 1]

Her responses would clearly seem to refuse him because he has already refused her. I do not mean in either case that the refusals are serious rejections; they are but part of a very real game of testing each other, of seeing how well they really understand each other. Words, after all, are only feeble expressions of real feeling. They embody a whole series of gestures that help spell out what is really meant. I take Millamant's injunction very seriously indeed— as, I think, she does:

Let us never visit together, nor go to a play together; but let us be very strange and well bred: let us be as strange as if we had been married a great while; and as well bred as if we were not married at all. [IV, 1]

It seems to me a surprisingly good, if difficult injunction to lay upon any marriage. It is, I think, the most serious moment in the whole scene, the conditions themselves to be agreed upon even as they are being given; and if these other conditions can be laughed off by Millamant and Mirabell rather than taken seriously, the underlying respect for and recognition of each other's independence is clear to both of them—and to us as well. To live together, a man and a woman need such respect. One must know that it is not words that convince (oaths are meaningless in Restoration comedy; only fools believe them to be binding), but the similarity of taste and desire that motivates those words. One remembers Dorimant's response to Mrs. Loveit when she criticizes him for recanting his vows of constancy: "I made 'em when I was in love." It is important in marriage that the pair understand language and what it represents in the same way. Sir Wilfull, who thinks Suckling a small pig, can never understand Millamant. It is not just her "lingo" that he cannot comprehend, but her tastes. It is partly because Mirabell can complete that Suckling couplet she quotes that she, and we, know that they can hear one another, know that they are on a similar wavelength.

This game of discovering each other's tastes is probably at its most serious—at least, it has its most important ramifications—in those encounters which lead toward marriage. The proviso scene is probably the most famous, but it is not unique. To be sure, in most such plays, the comparable scene is an attempt on the part of the man at simple seduction. Occasionally it leads toward marriage, as does the Dorimant–Harriet exchange in Act IV of Etherege's *The Man of Mode,* but as often it only leads toward bed as in the Archer–Mrs. Sullen tête-à-tête in *The Beaux' Stratagem* or that of Loveless and Berenthia in *The Relapse.* The important thing that language tells us is the kind of world the two would-be lovers discover with each other and their mutual recognition that it is the same world for both. Their wit is of interest to them and us, because it shows us that they are seeing the situation they are talking about in the same way and treating it with the same degree of seriousness. As one listens to Berenthia and Loveless in *The Relapse* come to terms with their desire for each other, it is important that each recognize the affair to be for temporary fun only, since Loveless is more or less happily married and Berenthia happily widowed. Listen to them sound each other out:

BERENTHIA   What makes you look so thoughtful, sir? I hope you are not ill.
LOVELESS   I was debating, Madam, whether I was so or not; and that was it which made me look so thoughtful.
BERENTHIA   Is it then so hard a matter to decide? I thought all people had been acquainted with their own bodies, though few people know their own minds.
LOVELESS   What if the distemper, I suspect, be in the mind?
BERENTHIA   Why, then I'll undertake to prescribe you a cure.
LOVELESS   Alas, you undertake you know not what.
BERENTHIA   So far at least then allow me to be a physician.
LOVELESS   Nay, I'll allow you so yet farther: for I have reason to believe, should I put myself into your hands you would increase my distemper.
BERENTHIA   Perhaps I might have reason from the college not to be too quick in your cure; but 'tis possible I might find ways to give you often ease, sir.
LOVELESS   Were I but sure of that, I'd quickly lay my case before you.
BERENTHIA   Whether you are sure of it or no, what risk do you run in trying?
LOVELESS   Oh, a very great one.
BERENTHIA   How?
LOVELESS   You might betray my distemper to my wife.
BERENTHIA   And so lose all my practice.
LOVELESS   Will you then keep my secret?
BERENTHIA   I will if you don't burst me.   [III, 2]

The scene continues but this is perhaps enough to suggest how it proceeds. The *double entendre* is fun in its own right to be sure, but theatrically it is that much more fun and that much more a pusher of the action if one recognizes that the characters are not only discussing the possibilities of an assignation but the terms under which it will operate. Not only are the symptoms wholly physical, but they may be cured wholly sexually. If Loveless fears that his disease is in the mind (where more than sexual complications might ensue), Berenthia assures him that her cure—" 'tis possible I might find ways to give you often ease"—is wholly physical. And his worry about his wife—a worry which is not only that she might discover the amour, but that Berenthia might wish such a discovery in order to make more of the affair—is nicely allayed in Berenthia's fear that in such betrayal she might "lose all [her] practice." Her only fear is pregnancy, again a physical not a spiritual problem. The scene continues with mutual oaths, but for Loveless on "Woman," his deity, and for Berenthia, "Man," her deity. No larger concerns than each other's physical delight for as long as the affair may last are involved here. There is nothing more holy than each other's pleasures, and a good deal of our delight in the scene is our recognition that both players in the love game know it. We know it because the playwright uses his language with care. I think it is important to note that it is not only that holy seventeenth-century trio Etherege, Wycherley, and Congreve who use it carefully, but Vanbrugh and Farquhar as well. Farquhar's world in *The Beaux' Stratagem,* for example, is not Congreve's world, but it is nevertheless a real world that Farquhar shows us, with a very hearable and definable tone of voice.

Let us look at *The Beaux' Stratagem* as a case in point. I think the whole play is built around the games the characters play, not only as lovers but simply as people who must cope with their existence. The center of the play, and the games the characters play to demonstrate the central concern, is the conviction on Farquhar's part that, given the energies of the human animal, it is hard, if not impossible, to chain him comfortably in an institution like marriage. For all the play's fun, it takes a very tough-minded look at the difficulty in maintaining an intelligent and comfortable relationship in marriage. The play may be saying that this adjustment is necessary primarily for the young, for certainly the play abounds with youth. On the other hand, there is nowhere in the play a suggestion that age might handle the difficulty any better. Age is simply not represented in the play, except in Lady Bountiful, a widow, and Boniface, a widower. Certainly what one is most struck by is the zest for life that abounds in all the characters, particularly in the two lead couples, and the problem of containing that zest without killing it. Love generates that zest. "You never talked so well in your life," says Mrs. Sullen to the younger Dorinda. "I was never in love before," she replies. But quite clearly, marriage kills that zest. The only time Mrs. Sullen and Squire Sullen have anything like a joyful conversation is when they play their little game of separation:

MRS. SULLEN   In the first place, I can't drink ale with him.
SQUIRE SULLEN   Nor can I drink tea with her.
MRS. SULLEN   I can't hunt with you.
SQUIRE SULLEN   Nor can I dance with you.
MRS. SULLEN   I hate cocking and racing.
SQUIRE SULLEN   And I abhor ombre and piquet.
MRS. SULLEN   Your silence is intolerable.
SQUIRE SULLEN   Your prating is worse.
MRS. SULLEN   Have we not been a perpetual offence to each other? a gnawing vulture at the heart?
SQUIRE SULLEN   A frightful goblin to the sight?
MRS. SULLEN   A porcupine to the feeling?
SQUIRE SULLEN   Perpetual wormwood to the taste?
MRS. SULLEN   Is there on earth a thing we could agree in?
SQUIRE SULLEN   Yes—to part.
MRS. SULLEN   With all my heart.
SQUIRE SULLEN   Your hand.
MRS. SULLEN   Here.
SQUIRE SULLEN   Those hands joined us, these shall part us.—Away!
MRS. SULLEN   North.
SQUIRE SULLEN   South.
MRS. SULLEN   East.
SQUIRE SULLEN   West—as far as the poles asunder.   [V, 5]

For the first time in the play, we hear the Sullens engaged in conversation with the same kind of delight that characterizes the rest of the characters throughout, unfettered as these others are by permanent alliances.

The play is made up of witty, put-on conversations that smack either of one-upmanship (if played by members of the same sex) or flirtations, with all the flattery and game-playing and dishonesty that flirtation implies (if played by members of the opposite sex). Nowhere do the characters talk seriously—that is to say, as if the issue they discussed were serious—except, as stated above, when they speak of marriage or as an already married couple. This is what one expects from the genre, of course. The whole archetypal pattern is of two lovers working their way toward marriage, the "gay couple" as they are often called. Since I believe that this progress is not only modern but, more important, available to modern actors and directors in production, I would like to look at some particular scenes and show how they outline playable and dramatic situations as well as point to a whole and consistent reading of the play.

If the play is still available to us as producible drama, it must be made up of situations that have immediate parallels in an actor's experience, not made up of some imagined idea of preciosity that could be labeled seventeenth-century fop, or a carefully wrought piece of baroque artistry called Millamant. If the play is drama as we understand drama, then it should be acted as we act drama, as confrontations that have their roots in real experience and their place in the play in the author's attempt to make sense of that experience. Plays, at least as we talk and write about them, seem to have something to say. If one talks of Jonson's *Volpone,* he speaks of the particular view of the human animal that Jonson presents to us—his stupidity, his greed, and his illusory sense (most clearly seen in Volpone and Mosca, but clearly true for the others as well) that he can rise above these limitations and control his destiny, be more than the limited fool Jonson insists he is. We do not say that any character in the play is "vastly entertaining, which is all anyone should expect from a comedy."

If *The Beaux' Stratagem* or any Restoration piece is good drama, one should be able to describe it in similar terms. The first scene I want to look at is between Dorinda and Mrs. Sullen:

MRS. SULLEN   Well, sister!
DORINDA   And well, sister!
MRS. SULLEN   What's become of my lord?
DORINDA   What's become of his servant?
MRS. SULLEN   Servant! He's a prettier fellow and a fine gentleman by fifty degrees than his master.
DORINDA   O' my conscience, I fancy you could beg that fellow at the gallow's-foot.
MRS. SULLEN   O' my conscience, I could, provided I could put a friend of yours in his room.
DORINDA   You desired me, sister, to leave you when you transgressed the bounds of honor.
MRS. SULLEN   You dear censorious country girl! what dost mean? You can't think of the man without the bedfellow, I find.
DORINDA   I don't find anything unnatural in that thought: while the mind is conversant with flesh and blood, it must conform to the humours of the company.

MRS. SULLEN How a little love and good company improves a woman! Why, child, you begin to live—you never spoke before.

DORINDA Because I was never spoke to.—My lord has told me that I have more wit and beauty than any of my sex; and truly I begin to think the man is sincere.

MRS. SULLEN You're in the right, Dorinda; pride is the life of a woman, and flattery is our daily bread; and she's a fool that won't believe a man there, as much as she that believes him in anything else. [IV, 1]

The scene between the two women takes place just after their first encounter with their young gentlemen: Aimwell, who would marry Dorinda; and Archer, who would seduce Mrs. Sullen. Clearly, Mrs. Sullen starts the attack with a sense of "And what have you been up to?" but when Dorinda counters it with the same attack, it would appear she is one-up on Mrs. Sullen, or at least ready to counter the attack. However much their defenses may have been down as they entered the unrecognized arena, they pop up quickly as the verbal exchange starts. They are able to cover the dangerous condition of being vulnerable in a hurry. The scene continues in what could be read as a serious fight but appears, given the stakes and the already established intimacy of the two, to be a game of one-upmanship. It's a game that Dorinda seems to win at first. Through the first four lines, certainly, it is she who mocks Mrs. Sullen in the repetition of phrases, and it is Mrs. Sullen who seems to retreat in some confusion, in her "Servant! He's a prettier fellow." It even looks as if Dorinda has won as she moves in confidently, no longer repeating Mrs. Sullen's accusations but beginning her own with her "O' my conscience." It is only when we hear Mrs. Sullen's return, now using Dorinda's repetition tactics, that we suspect Dorinda may have walked into a trap. The trap, of course, is to admit that one has lost control, and that is what Dorinda does when in some shock she says, "You desired me, sister, to leave you when you transgressed the bounds of honor," apparently too shocked to continue, and hence defeated.

Her exit is stopped by Mrs. Sullen, who laughingly points out that Dorinda has lost, only to be finally topped by Dorinda's beautiful rejoinder that even Mrs. Sullen must admit defeats her. The phrasing is delicious, and shows us something of this young lady's awakening to her own vitality. And though the comment, in its admission of her interest in men, is by that very fact a surrender, it is a surrender so nicely phrased that Mrs. Sullen must applaud with her "Why, child, you begin to live—you never spoke before." It is a delightful speech because it is a retreat that says "Let's not play at being angry any more; let's admit we both like men and play the next game that appears in the script, namely, which man is the better wooer." The speech shows that Dorinda is perfectly willing to admit her feelings, but in the way she phrases those feelings she also shows us that she is not, at least as yet, mastered by them: "while the mind is conversant with flesh and blood, it must conform to the humours of the company." This is no priggish statement of high-flown but unsupportable philosophizing; it is in fact a mockery of such a position. Certainly the vocabulary, the "conversant with flesh and blood," suggests a philosophical or moral sermon, but the conclusion mocks any such preachment. We do not hear something like "indulge in their necessities," which says much the same thing but completes the priggish attitude with which the speech began. One suspects Dorinda is almost as delighted and surprised at her ability to talk as is Mrs. Sullen. She is coming of age; and though her connection to Aimwell at the end of the play is not yet a mature one (I think she is a little too much in love when she marries him to see straight), it does suggest the awakening involved in falling in love, if not the dangers.

There are many such games in the play. The Dorinda–Mrs. Sullen scene is basically one-upmanship. There are others: Gibbet playing suave highwayman on his first entrance, where he demonstrates his brilliance at derring-do. Certainly one cannot take the following speech as a serious description of the occupation of thievery:

No matter, ask no questions, all fair and honorable—Here, my good Cherry.—[*Gives her a bag.*] Two hundred sterling pounds, as good as any that ever hanged or saved a rogue; lay 'em by with the rest; and here—three wedding or mourning rings, 'tis much the same, you know—here, two silver-hilted swords; I took those from fellows that never show any part of the swords but the hilts—here is a diamond necklace which the lady hid in the privatest place in the coach, but I found it out—this gold watch I took from a pawnbroker's wife; it was left in her hands by a person of quality, there's the arms upon the case. [II, 3]

The speech is a strut for Gibbet, a chance to show off. It is not just information he is presenting, but himself—and with a flourish. He is not as committed to robbery as he is to the way of doing it.

Throughout the play we are struck by people defending their activities with a kind of posture that always allows them a way out. They refuse to take themselves seriously.

Perhaps the most obvious games are those between Archer and Mrs. Sullen and between Cherry and Archer. The Archer–Mrs. Sullen scenes are fairly straightforward. Archer speaks and acts like some eighteenth-century Errol Flynn, and while Mrs. Sullen knows his compliments are for the fun of it, she finds him irresistible, not for love but for joy:

MRS. SULLEN   Pray, sir, what head is that in the corner there?
ARCHER   O Madam, 'tis poor Ovid in his exile.
MRS. SULLEN   What was he banished for?
ARCHER   His ambitious love, Madam.—[Bowing] His misfortune touches me.
MRS. SULLEN   Was he successful in his amours?
ARCHER   There he has left us in the dark.—He was too much a gentleman to tell.
MRS. SULLEN   If he were secret, I pity him.
ARCHER   And if he were successful, I envy him.
MRS. SULLEN   How d'ye like that Venus over the chimney?
ARCHER   Venus! I protest, Madam, I took it for your picture; but now I look again, 'tis not handsome enough.
MRS. SULLEN   Oh, what a charm is flattery!   [IV, 1]

The delight that Mrs. Sullen takes in leading Archer on with her "Was he successful in his amours?" and again, "If he were secret, I pity him," only to lead him off with her "How d'ye like that Venus over the chimney?" suggests something far less intense than the blind rapture with which Dorinda and Aimwell are examining the picture.

Dorinda and Aimwell do not play games in their wooing. They take each other very seriously; it is, in fact, one of their limitations for Farquhar; and we are asked, I think, to recognize their pink haze and to laugh at it. Love may be very moving, but it is also blind—and neither Mrs. Sullen and Archer nor Cherry and Archer are ever blind or unaware of what they are doing. The conversations here are self-conscious, and the participants are perfectly aware of what they are doing and where it might lead—the delights and the dangers. The picture scene is an excellent example of both the awareness of Mrs. Sullen and Archer and the blindness of Dorinda and Aimwell. The latter do not even see the pictures.

They try, but obviously their eyes can see only each other. The former couple are quite aware of the pictures and of where a close scrutiny of them might lead. Archer is headed for the bedroom, and Mrs. Sullen knows it. She has the contradictory task of leading him away from the obvious and yet not away from her—as Gay says, "By keeping men off, we keep them on."

It is Mrs. Sullen's self-awareness of how she has led Archer on that keeps the later near rape scene (V, 3) from being unpleasant. Her pleas for help are less and less persuasive to both Archer and herself. We must see, regardless of the words, her gradual melting into Archer's embrace. And I suspect her last "Thieves! Thieves! Murder!" is about as loud as Berenthia's whispered "Rape!" in Vanbrugh's *The Relapse*. Certainly it is not her screams that have brought Scrub running, though Archer can first understand his appearance in no other way. The fact is that Scrub has seen thieves; he is in no way aware of what is going on in Mrs. Sullen's bedroom. Mrs. Sullen is playing the age-old game of saying "no" when she means "yes," and Archer, the age-old game of saying "I love you" when he means "I want you." The important thing to recognize here is that both of them know it. There is no self-delusion about "True love overcomes all" or "This is too big for both of us." Mrs. Sullen may repent of what she is doing—indeed, she does—but there is no cry of "I have been betrayed" or "You have taken advantage of me." Her only criticism of Archer, in the last scene of the play just before the arrival of her brother, is that he is a little cold-blooded and bad-mannered about his proposition now. He must keep up the appearances of wooing even if he doesn't mean it, or she cannot keep up the pretense of being a lady.

The Cherry–Archer scenes are much the same, but the game here is so obvious, so nearly danced, that there is a tendency in production to "dance" it, to make it an entertainment in its own right with no reference to the event it delineates. Their second scene (II, 3) is the most formal, since it is in the form of a skit to be played by Cherry for Archer, starting with Archer's line, "Come, come, my dear, have you conned over the catechism I taught you last night?" and ending with "Hold, hold, Mr. Martin." The sequence of the scene is much like the Archer–Mrs. Sullen scene in the picture gallery. Archer, disguised here as Martin, would lead Cherry to the bed chamber; and Cherry is even more ready than Mrs. Sullen to go—that is the reason she has learned "love's catechism" and repeats it as charmingly as possible (and, I might add, with the same touch of refusal that the lines suggest). Cherry, as she admits later in the scene, wants to marry a gentleman; and she thinks Archer is one. As a consequence, she is using the catechism as a come-on, but coyly. The lover must "desire much and hope little," "he must adore the person that disdains him," and so on. In other words, the wooing game must be played, and Cherry knows it. I think that, in doing the scene, Cherry simply cannot play the putting-off with the lines alone. Perhaps she enters with an armful of sheets which she might make Archer help her fold as she recites, and behind which she could duck to avoid, or peep over to receive, any kisses that the script says she must deal with. Somehow the whole recital is too naked a compliance with Archer's request, and makes her too easy a conquest. The making him work for her gives her back just enough of her own to keep the game from being too one-sided.

Farquhar's world, at least insofar as it includes the relations between the sexes, is a game-playing world, made up of healthy animals of sound body and quick mind who, when they drop their conviction that any relationship between them must be casual, careful, friendly, and uncommitted, become a little silly (the falling in love of Dorinda and Aimwell) or a little vicious (the marriage of Squire Sullen and Mrs. Sullen). There is no delight in the relationship between Sullen and his wife, and I think it demonstrable that Aimwell and Dorinda, though occasionally charming, are also to be laughed at. Aimwell is, in fact, continually chastised by Archer for his tendency to ruin things by falling in love, and he is finally rather seriously attacked by Archer when it looks as if all is lost. His weakness is his heart, his sentimental nature. Dorinda's weakness is slightly different. She is innocent, an innocent who is waking up, to be sure, but in the course of this play only waking up to the joys of love, not to its dangers. In her scene with Mrs. Sullen, quoted below, in which she tries to duel verbally, she continually comes close to losing, finally being saved only by her insistence that her fellow asked for her hand:

MRS. SULLEN . . . But I'll lay you a guinea that I had finer things said to me than you had.
DORINDA Done! What did your fellow say to ye?

MRS. SULLEN   My fellow took the picture of Venus for mine.
DORINDA   But my lover took me for Venus herself.
MRS. SULLEN   Common cant! Had my spark called me a Venus directly, I should have believed him a footman in good earnest.
DORINDA   But my lover was upon his knees to me.
MRS. SULLEN   And mine was upon his tiptoes to me.
DORINDA   Mine vowed to die for me.
MRS. SULLEN   Mine vowed to die with me.
DORINDA   Mine spoke the softest moving things.
MRS. SULLEN   Mine had his moving things too.
DORINDA   Mine kissed my hand ten thousand times.
MRS. SULLEN   Mine has all that pleasure to come.
DORINDA   Mine offered marriage.
MRS. SULLEN   O Lard! d'ye call that a moving thing?
DORINDA   The sharpest arrow in his quiver, my dear Sister! Why, my ten thousand pounds may lie brooding here this seven years, and hatch nothing at last but some ill-natured clown like yours! Whereas, if I marry my Lord Aimwell, there will be title, place, and precedence, the Park, the play, and the drawing-room, splendor, equipage, noise, and flambeaux.—*Hey, my Lady Aimwell's servants there!—Lights, lights to the stairs!—My Lady Aimwell's coach put forward!—Stand by, make room for her ladyship!*—Are not these things moving?—   [IV, 1]

She is not up to Mrs. Sullen's *double entendre.* I suspect she can understand it; but it is not the kind of compliment that charms her, since what she sees in marriage is herself as Lady Aimwell with all the attendant social pleasures. One cannot say with any certainty that she will never have these pleasures, but one can imagine Mrs. Sullen having seen the same world before she got married. There is a certain illusory quality in Dorinda's vision of being Lady Aimwell and her assurance that she will have "title, place, and precedence," especially when one remembers that the man she is talking about marrying is the younger brother of Lord Aimwell, not Lord Aimwell himself. The sense of that blindness is also carried out in the relationship between Aimwell and Dorinda. Not only is this apparent in their gazing at each other in the picture-gallery scene, but in the near marriage late in the play. It is here that Farquhar most obviously tips his hand, I think, and makes clear that his sympathies are not entirely with Aimwell and Dorinda:

DORINDA   Well, well, my lord, you have conquered; your late generous action will, I hope, plead for my easy yielding; though I must own, your lordship had a friend in the fort before.
AIMWELL   The sweets of Hybla dwell upon her tongue. Here doctor.

[FOIGARD *enters.*]

FOIGARD   Are you prepared both?

DORINDA   I'm ready. But first, my lord, one word—I have a frightful example of a hasty marriage in my own family; when I reflect upon't, it shocks me. Pray, my lord, consider a little—

AIMWELL   Consider! do you doubt my honor or my love?

DORINDA   Neither! I do believe you equally just as brave and were your whole sex drawn out for me to choose, I should not cast a look upon the multitude if you were absent. But, my lord, I'm a woman; colours, concealments may hide a thousand faults in me; therefore know me better first. I hardly dare affirm I know myself, in anything except my love.

AIMWELL [*aside*]   Such goodness who could injure! I find myself unequal to the task of villain; she has gained my soul, and made it honest like her own. I—cannot hurt her.—[*Aloud*] Doctor, retire.—

[FOIGARD *exits.*]

Madam, behold your lover and your proselyte, and judge of my passion by my conversion!—I'm all a lie, nor dare I give a fiction to your arms; I'm all counterfeit, except my passion.

DORINDA   Forbid it, Heaven! a counterfeit!

AIMWELL   I am no lord, but a poor needy man, come with a mean, a scandalous design to prey upon your fortune; but the beauties of your mind and person have so won me from myself that, like a trusty servant, I prefer the interest of my mistress to my own.

DORINDA   Sure I have had the dream of some poor mariner, a sleepy image of a welcome port, and wake involved in storms!—Pray, sir, who are you?

AIMWELL   Brother to the man whose title I usurped, but stranger to his honor or his fortune.

DORINDA   Matchless honesty!—Once I was proud, sir, of your wealth and title, but now I am prouder that you want it: now I can show my love was justly levelled, and has no aim but love. Doctor, come in.

[FOIGARD *reenters. Simultaneously,* GIPSY *comes in and whispers to* DORINDA.]

Your pardon, sir, we shannot want you now. [*To* AIMWELL] Sir, you must excuse me—I'll wait upon you presently. [DORINDA *exits with* GIPSY.]

FOIGARD   Upon my shoul, now, dis is foolish. [V, 5]

The most obvious thing in the scene, demonstrated most particularly in the way Foigard is handled, is that Farquhar is consciously laughing at the marriage. The continual interruptions to dismiss or recall the comic priest; his necessary comic confusions and suspicions as he wonders whether he is to marry the couple or not; and finally, a little later, Archer's command to him to "Make haste, make haste, couple 'em anyway" cannot help but suggest a lack of seriousness in the coupling. There is something silly about marriage based on such flimsy foundations as the clichéd kind of true love that we see here. One is persuaded not only by the farcical coming and going of the priest, but by such a line as Dorinda's "Sure I have had the dream of some poor mariner, a sleepy image of a welcome port, and wake involved in storms! Pray, sir, who are you?" No matter how seriously this is delivered, one is struck with the self-consciousness of the metaphor which must take one a little away from a completely personal and heartfelt response on Dorinda's part. There is something precious here that is a comment on the situation. The language qualifies the emotion as surely as Alceste's rhymed couplets qualify his anger. Such evidence by itself might simply be proof of bad writing, but given the use of Foigard throughout the play, the comic Irishman with a brogue trying to be a Frenchman; Farquhar's general distrust of marriage throughout the play; and the *deus ex machina* arrival of Sir Charles Freeman with his announcement of Aimwell's sudden inheritance of his brother's title, I think a pretty good case can be made to suggest Farquhar's awareness of the limitations of the kind of foundation upon which Dorinda and Aimwell are basing their happiness. Here is Sir Charles arriving with the news:

SIR CHARLES My dear Lord Aimwell, I wish you joy.
AIMWELL Of what?
SIR CHARLES Of your honor and estate. Your brother died the day before I left London; and all your friends have writ after you to Brussels—among the rest I did myself the honor.
ARCHER Hark'ee, Sir Knight, don't you banter now?
SIR CHARLES 'Tis truth, upon my honor.
AIMWELL Thanks to the pregnant stars that formed this accident.
ARCHER Thanks to the womb of time that brought it forth!—away with it!
AIMWELL [*to* DORINDA] Thanks to my guardian angel that led me to the prize!
ARCHER And double thanks to the noble Sir Charles Freeman.—My Lord, I wish you joy. My lady, I wish you joy.—Egad, Sir Charles Freeman, You're the honestest fellow living! 'Sdeath, I'm grown strange airy upon this matter! [V, 5]

The grammatical parallelism of their responses suggests a playful dance that winds up a theatrical entertainment, rather than a believable or convincing solution to the problem presented. Such accidents as Lord Aimwell's death are hardly worth assuming in making a marriage arrangement, and I don't think Farquhar is any more convinced than I am that true love has done any more than help to end the play. Farquhar is as aware of the contrivance as Shakespeare is in *Twelfth Night* and uses it to much the same purpose. The accidents that end *Twelfth Night* suggest not the accident of successful marriage, with which the play does not deal, but the accident of falling in love. So here, the accident of sudden wealth in no way saves what was previously unhealthy without it. Until Dorinda and Aimwell get down to earth, one can't evaluate their future. Their present is in a pink haze, to which money is a joyful addition. There is no suggestion that it is a salvation.

I think the play not only is very well put together, but makes a very real comment on the difficulty, if not the impossibility, of committing oneself to one love, to one person. Such commitment denies change, which would seem a necessary part of man's interest in the opposite sex. It is feasible, it would seem, if one could remain in that pink haze that surrounds Aimwell and Dorinda, but I don't think Farquhar has any great trust in the continuance of such a state for long. Certainly he chuckles at it while it's going on. Throughout the play, however, the most compelling interest in scene after scene is the ebullient and effervescent life that comes from these lovers, an ebullience that seems to thrive on novelty, on a new conquest, on a new man or a new woman. And what seems to feed this life is man's refusal to commit himself to one view of the world, his need to look elsewhere. I think it is the games these people play and the zest with which they play them that demonstrate this conviction of mine, and I think it is the care with which Farquhar phrases those games that make my defense possible.

As one moves on into the eighteenth century, it becomes increasingly difficult both to be sure of what the playwright is saying and to pin down with any exactness what the game is. Even Sheridan, who is I think more defensible as a good playwright than his immediate predecessors, is difficult to pin down. It is easy enough to enjoy particular moments in, say, *The School for Scandal;* it is not so easy to add them up to much. In the first place, his central characters are much less interesting than those in the earlier plays mentioned here. Why do so many producers ignore Maria in the play and stress Lady Teazle? Structurally, Lady Teazle is the fool

(*The Country Wife's* Margery or *Love for Love's* Prue), not the admired norm of the play. Our sympathies (those that go to Mrs. Sullen or Millamant) should go to Maria, but she usually disappears in production. Charles, the Mirabell or Archer of the piece, keeps his place of importance, but the shape of the play is twisted. So too, I think, are the games to be played and the language in which they are played.

Let me look at two of the most important scenes in the play: the first gossip scene, and the screen scene. What is of most importance to note is that neither of the two are games at all, that is, a playing at something other than what is apparent. It is, in fact, this feature which makes the play so immediately available to actors and hence to audiences. There are no hidden workings here. There is no proviso scene which really is an engagement party, there is no conversation about disease which is really a seduction, there is no conversation about pictures which is really a game of one-upmanship. In *The School for Scandal* a gossip scene is a gossip scene. It has no other point than to make gossip as brilliant as possible.

If one compares it to its most obvious counterpart in *The Way of the World,* one must look at that scene in which Millamant first appears on stage. Her entrance is into St. James' Park surrounded by her admirers. "Here she comes," says Mirabell, "full sail, with her fan spread and her streamers out, and a shoal of fools for tenders." As one listens to Witwoud drop his would-be *bon mots,* one is aware that, like the gossip scene, part of the charm here is Witwoud's talk:

MIRABELL   You seem to be unattended, madam—you used to have the *beau monde* throng after you; and a flock of gay fine perukes hovering round you.
WITWOUD   Like moths about a candle.—I had like to have lost my comparison for want of breath.
MIRABELL   O I have denied myself airs to-day, I have walked as fast through the crowd.
WITWOUD   As a favourite just disgraced; and with as few followers.
MILLAMANT   Dear Mr. Witwoud, truce with your similitudes; for I'm as sick of 'em—
WITWOUD   As a physician of a good air.—I cannot help it, madam, though 'tis against myself.   [II, 2]

To be sure, we are made aware of his limitations, but part of our laughter is directed at his ability to find the apt phrase, even though its application is against himself. We are also aware, however, that the scene is basically Witwoud's attempt at flirtation, his attempt to persuade Millamant of his brilliance. It is a failure surely, but his attempt to impress Millamant and her rejection of him are examples of those games the sexes play with each other in their courting. Mirabell's continuation of the game demonstrates the same thing, though admittedly he is a little better at it.

My point here is that the event, so clear in *The School for Scandal*, is much less clear in Congreve's play, even though Congreve's scene is much more a part of his play which, after all, concerns the wooing, by almost everyone, of Millamant. The gossip scene in *The School for Scandal* is much easier to play on stage, because it is so much more obvious to anyone what it is. Its only limitation is that it doesn't get us any farther into the action of the play. We do get a chance to see the brilliance of Lady Teazle (not Maria), but at the service of nothing in particular. She shines for her own sake, unlike Millamant, who performs equally brilliantly but manages at the same time to show us and her suitors how well she can control them. And this lack of focus is reflected in the two playwrights' use of language. Witwoud's similes have a certain verbal delight in their own right, but they are means of delineating Witwoud's character as well, and of demonstrating his inability to communicate with Millamant. A turn of phrase he may manage, but the wit to know when to turn it is not his. Our laughter results as much from this deficiency in Witwoud as from the phrases themselves.

The same is not true of Sheridan. The verbal sheen is there, but it works differently. Here is an example from the gossip scene:

CRABTREE   Oh, to be sure! she has herself the oddest countenance that ever was seen; 'tis a collection of features from all the different countries of the globe.
BENJAMIN   So she has, indeed—an Irish front!
CRABTREE   Caledonian locks!
BENJAMIN   Dutch nose!
CRABTREE   Austrian lips!
BENJAMIN   Complexion of a Spaniard!
CRABTREE   And teeth *à la Chinoise!*

BENJAMIN In short, her face resembles a *table d'hôte* at Spa—where no two guests are of a nation—
CRABTREE Or a congress at the close of a general war—wherein all the members, even to her eyes, appear to have a different interest, and her nose and chin are the only parties likely to join issue. [II, 2]

This is wonderful badinage, more fun to listen to than Witwoud's witticisms, but there is no attempt to create any character out of the comments, nor is there any specific situation with which they must cope. Sir Benjamin and Crabtree are similar voices. Their jests are of a piece. The same cannot be said of Witwoud and Petulant who are both would-be wits, but entirely different people. Sheridan's witty dialogue is frankly to amuse; it attempts nothing more. Character slips in where it may. Put Charles against Mirabell or Lady Teazle against Millamant as their language defines them as people, and Sheridan's characters are thin indeed. But see Lady Teazle behind a screen or listen to the gossips destroy their friends, watch Charles sell off his relatives to Sir Oliver, and I fear you tend to forget the whole character.

The screen scene is another but different change from similar scenes in previous comedies. The scene begins with Sir Joseph's attempt to seduce Lady Teazle by overcoming "the ill effects of her country education" and persuading her that an affair with him would remove "the consciousness of her innocence" which continually makes her impatient of Sir Peter's temper and thoughtless in her conduct. The lesson is interrupted by the arrival of Sir Peter, and Joseph is forced to hide the lady. The comparable scenes in the late seventeenth- and early eighteenth-century comedies would be those in which Berenthia capitulated to Loveless, Margery to Horner, or Prue to Tattle. Normally the scene ends off-stage or like this one is interrupted by an untimely arrival—the robbery in *The Beaux' Stratagem* which interrupts Archer at the crucial moment or even Lady Freelove's interruption of Trinket's attempt on Harriet in as late a piece as *The Jealous Wife*. In Sheridan's play the interruption comes earlier than in comparable plays and is perhaps a little more delicate, but then most of the people in *The School for Scandal* are talkers not doers. I am not here quarreling about Sheridan's taste or his delicacy, but his technique. The comparable scenes earlier make their point in the conversation between two principals, and the climax of the scene is the culmination or interruption of the seduction. This is not the case in *The School for Scandal.* The climax is Joseph operating at his hypocritical and amusing best after Lady Teazle is hidden; in fact, it really comes to a climax when both Lady Teazle and Sir Peter are hidden as a third party, Charles Surface, arrives. Here is Joseph, with the screen and Lady Teazle on one side of him, the closet and Sir Peter on the other:

SIR PETER   Sly rogue! sly rogue! [*Goes into closet.*]
JOSEPH SURFACE   A narrow escape, indeed! and a curious situation I'm in, to part man and wife in this manner.
LADY TEAZLE [*peeping from the screen*]   Couldn't I steal off?
JOSEPH SURFACE   Keep close, my angel.
SIR PETER [*peeping*]   Joseph, tax him home!
JOSEPH SURFACE   Back, my dear friend!
LADY TEAZLE [*peeping out*]   Couldn't you lock Sir Peter in?
JOSEPH SURFACE   Be still, my life!
SIR PETER [*peeping*]   You're sure the little milliner won't blab?
JOSEPH SURFACE   In, in, my dear Sir Peter!—'Fore Gad, I wish I had a key to the door!   [IV, 3]

The scene is not brilliant verbal wit, but if one can imagine the takes of relief and then fear on poor Joseph's face or the tensions in his body as from either side Lady Teazle and Sir Peter question him, almost discovering each other in every intance, one can begin to *see* Joseph's hypocrisy closing in on him. It is not only the false sound of his sentiments that delineates his double face. Here we see it in operation—one mask for Lady Teazle and one for Sir Peter. And neither mask is as clear a delineator of the real Joseph as is the harried look of fear and confusion that must appear between peeps.

The gossip scene and the screen scene demonstrate, I think, a direction that theatre through the nineteenth century was to take. Obviously, this generalization is dangerous and probably demonstrably qualifiable at least. But one notes in plays after Sheridan an increasing interest in the visual, and part of being a good playwright and producer in the nineteenth century was the talent to exploit this interest thoroughly. The large theatres, the increasing use of stage machinery, the melodrama's interest in spectacle, are all examples of both the interest and its implications. I mention it here not to suggest a source for the change, but to point out an aspect of theatre that Congreve, Etherege, even Farquhar and Vanbrugh did not worry too much about. The big scenes in the play are obvious, not only explicitly visual (Imagine Charles selling his pictures without the pictures!) but, because they embody an action that is explicit and easily actable, demonstrable. An auction is a commonplace occurrence. A producer has no trouble recognizing the event here and hence recreating it on stage. The game is obvious to anyone. Etherege, speaking as he did to a near intimate five hundred friends, could be much tighter in his presentation of the way people flirt than could Vanbrugh and Farquhar. By "tighter" I mean he could make private "in" jokes, he could trust much more to an "in" audience than even Vanbrugh and Farquhar could, who had to write for London at large, not for Charles II and his friends. One can write a school review which is a howling success to members of the school but a complete mystery to outsiders, and Vanbrugh was writing to outsiders. The *double entendre* in *The Relapse* between Berenthia and Loveless makes the seduction much easier to recognize than Dorimant's attempts in his first meeting with Harriet. In Sheridan's play even this much camouflage has been removed, and the focus has been put elsewhere, where it can be seen. Conversation here is for its glitter, its wit alone, not for its ability to characterize. Language is literally used to delight us for its own sake, not simply to help propel the action.

CHAPTER IV

V

Chekhov: A New View of Language

The history of English drama during the nineteenth and early twentieth century and finally of American drama is in many ways the history of those factors in theatre other than language which can be, and indeed are, exploited for theatrical effect. As theatre equipment grows in complexity, as visual effects become more immediately graphic, as lighting, particularly, becomes more refined in the kinds of effects it can achieve, and ultimately as the motion picture becomes a substitute for popular theatre, language as a controlling factor in drama becomes less precise. It is indeed less important, so much so that by 1930 in America, Sydney Howard could say that his plays were only scenarios for actors and their written form was never sure until actors had improvised upon his initial efforts.

Though "collapse" is a loaded and probably silly description, certainly a change in the precision with which language defines situation and character can be seen as early as 1775. When one compares Sheridan's *The School for Scandal* to the work of Congreve, it is not only the social mores, the kinds of protagonists admired, that have changed. For whatever reasons—Sheridan's talents, the theatre's demands, society's interests—language in this play makes its points and its jokes in a different way than it does in Congreve. Sheridan is a visual playwright; that is, he is aware of the value of writing scenes one can see as well as hear. The kind of action that language can create is quite simply of less interest to him, and I would say that this direction away from such interest is even more pronounced in the nineteenth century. Language as a carefully used tool for the actor almost disappears in England until the arrival of Shaw and Wilde, or perhaps Robertson. What is developing in drama is what we now call the melodrama, a visual theatre with musical accompaniment, the forerunner to the modern movie. Listen to the climactic moments in three such plays.

Here is the final curtain of *The Forest Oracle*, 1829, as quoted in Nicoll, *History of English Drama*, Vol. 4:

[*He rushes down, followed by* ARANZA, AARON, *and party, with torches—general fight—*FILIPPO *catches the* CHILD, *and throws it in the torrent—*DELZI *knocks him down, and, mounting the bridge, looks anxiously after it—jumps in—two* MEN *fire after him—*FILIPPO *beckons two others, who ascend the bridge, and fire—*AARON, *who has received a whisper from* ADRIANI, *seizes a torch, and, firing the train, the bridge blows up with a tremendous explosion—all are struck motionless—*DELZI *is seen coming through the ruins with the* CHILD—*he places it in its parents' arms—*COLONNA *rushes forward to stab it, when* DELZI, *catching his poniard, stabs him—the* FILIPPO *party are conquered—Picture—Curtain falls.*]

Here is a more poetic but equally pictorial curtain in *Giselle* by Moncrieff in 1841, as quoted in Nicoll, *History of English Drama*, Vol. 4:

[*The Dell of the Mist in the Forest of Rosenbad; a romantic thicket; wild shrubs and flowers thickly bestrew the ground; the silvery mist of the morning is seen ascending in natural incense from the earth, gilded by the first rays of the rising sun, which is brightly piercing through the forest verdure, at the back, chasing the shades of night, and lighting up the dewdrops with its beams like fairy lamps.—Supernatural Music.—*LOTTA *and* WILLIS *enter, slowly waltzing onwards, their movements becoming fainter and weaker, as the Sun's rays beam more strongly, 'till, staggering and apparently dying away, they disappear through the tufts of flowers at the wings.*]

And finally this description of "real life" as early as 1834 in *The Scamps of London* by Moncrieff, as quoted in Nicoll, *History of English Drama*, Vol. 4:

[CHARLOTTE *has rushed to* BOB—LOUISA *to* HERBERT—*and* ELIZA, *encouraged by her* FATHER *to* FRANK. *A desperate Combat then takes place between* POLICE, *headed by* FOGG, *and* ONION, BRINDLE, *and* SCAMPS, *headed by* DEVEREUX—*the* POLICE *hastening to secure them—pistols are fired—cutlasses crossed, 'til* ONION *and* SCAMPS *are conquered by the* POLICE; *and* DEVEREUX *receives a pistol shot from* FOGG, *who has wrested it from him in the struggle, when levelled at his own head, and, in self-*

defence, has lodged the contents of it in DEVEREUX'S body, it stretches him lifeless on the ground—with his last breath he makes a motion as if imploring pardon. FOGG regards him with great agitation, then turns away, as if in forgiveness, and raises his eyes to heaven in grateful thanks —he then sinks into his daughter's arms, who leaves HERBERT to support him. SHABNER has sneaked off in the confusion—Parties form Tableau and Curtain falls.]

One finally is not surprised at the following description of the Haymarket theatre in London in 1881, by Percy Fitzgerald, *The World Behind the Scenes*, as quoted in Nicoll, *History of English Drama*, Vol. 4:

A rich and elaborate gold border, about two feet broad, after the pattern of a picture frame, is continued all round the proscenium and carried even below the actor's feet—There can be no doubt the sense of illusion is increased, and for the reason just given; the actors seem cut off from the domain of prose; there is no borderline of platform in front; and, stranger still, the whole has the air of a picture projected on a surface.

Although the great growth of the visual, the picturing of the event, is crucial to the growth of nineteenth-century drama in England, words are still there. They are subsidiary in most successful playwrights' vision, and indeed the nineteenth century finds them a problem, at least until the advent of something like realistic dialogue. There was, after all, an already established mode of serious theatrical expression growing out of Shakespeare and his contemporaries. Verse had always been the correct and meaningful way to deal with human experience on a stage, if one meant to deal with it seriously. To be sure, since Lillo's *The London Merchant* in 1731, playwrights had been working toward some way to use realistic prose, but "serious" writers through Coleridge and Knowles and even Bulwer-Lytton, to name only those we may still hear of, were working diligently in verse. Coleridge, despite his ability as a poet, never really understood the theatre, nor cared to; he hoped to make a little money out of it. Knowles and Bulwer-Lytton, who did understand the theatre, got caught someplace between their desire to write in an acceptable declamatory style they called verse and their recognition, conscious or unconscious, that it was almost impossible to get such language into the ever-increasingly detailed and realistic decoration the stage could and did now give them.

Bulwer-Lytton, particularly, it seems to me, lets us hear a sense of humor in his blank verse that denies its seriousness. At its best it laughs at itself, swashbuckling gloriously through Richelieu's France, for example; but unfortunately there is invariably that moment when it must take itself seriously, and here it fails. The delight in such fustian is still with us—I suppose Maxwell Anderson is bombast's best-known American exponent—but unfortunately the playwright who uses it always takes himself more seriously than the verse will allow him. Critics cried throughout the nineteenth century for the return of poetry. What they got, finally, was someone who could use prose with the precision of poetry.

That man was Chekhov. It was Chekhov not because he was the first man to use realistic dialogue seriously and successfully (Ibsen and Shaw had done this), but because he was the first playwright to use such conversation in a new structure that allowed it to speak in a new way. Shaw's greatest service to the theatre is to remind us that language, handled with care, can still make very telling theatrical statements. How good it is to listen to him! But his plays, like his prose, are still terribly "well-made." Scribe's artificiality still hangs on him. For all his laughter at Sardoodelum, there is still in Shaw's plays a similar kind of theatricalism in both his curtains and his prose.

Listen to *Caesar and Cleopatra*, end of Act I:

CAESAR   Now if you quail—[*He seats himself on the throne.*]

[*She stands on the step, all but unconscious, waiting for death. The Roman soldiers troop in tumultuously through the corridor, headed by their ensign with his eagle, and their bucinator, a burly fellow with his instrument coiled round his body, its brazen bell shaped like the head of a howling wolf. When they reach the transept, they stare in amazement at the throne; dress into ordered rank opposite it; draw their swords and lift them in the air with a shout of*] Hail Caesar.

[CLEOPATRA *turns and stares wildly at* CAESAR; *grasps the situation; and, with a great sob of relief, falls into his arms.*]

The final curtain in *Candida:*

MARCHBANKS   . . . Let me go now. The night outside grows impatient.
CANDIDA   Goodbye. [*She takes his face in her hands; and as he divines her intention and falls on his knees, she kisses his forehead. Then he*

flies out into the night. She turns to MORELL, *holding out her arms to him.*] Ah, James!

[*They embrace. But they do not know the secret in the poet's heart.*]

Misalliance, final curtain (the speaker, Tarleton, you must remember has been the great talker, the great truth-giver-out-of-books throughout the play) :

TARLETON   Well, I—er [*He addresses* LINA, *and stops.*] I—er [*He addresses* LORD SUMMERHAYS, *and stops.*] I—er [*He gives up.*] Well, I suppose—er— I suppose there's nothing more to be said.
HYPATIA [*fervently*]   Thank goodness!

The final curtain of *Saint Joan:*

[*The last remaining rays of light gather into a white radiance descending on* JOAN. *The hour continues to strike.*]

JOAN   O God that madest this beautiful earth, when will it be ready to receive Thy saints? How long, O Lord, how long?

I suppose *Saint Joan* and *Caesar* might qualify as somehow historical, but they are also typical. *Pygmalion,* almost alone of Shaw's good plays, ends with a less theatrical, simple pointing at the situation he has developed.

I don't argue with the effectiveness of any of them, but I can't get away from Shaw's contrivance at gaining that effect. When he is going well, as I think he is in *Pygmalion* or *Man and Superman* or *Caesar and Cleopatra,* he is telling us something important about the relationship of men and women, but he owes as much or more to Congreve and Etherege as to anything we might call realism. Listen to Ann and Jack at the end of *Man and Superman:*

ANN [*looking at him with fond pride and caressing his arm*]   Never mind her, dear. Go on talking.
TANNER   Talking!

[*Universal laughter.*]

It's almost like a couplet out of a Restoration comedy of manners. The proper young man has finally captured (or been captured by) the proper young woman. We have been given some insight into how that relationship has worked, does work, and will work, and now to conclude let's have a wedding dance. The form is already there for Shaw and, though he shapes it somewhat to fit his purposes, it is not new.[1] Shaw's plays like Congreve's or Etherege's are still traditionally structured; that is, they are kept going by their attention to the change in point of view about how the world works in a central character (Dorimant in *The Man of Mode*, Eliza in *Pygmalion*) or by their attention to an expected but cleverly manipulated story line (How will Valentine catch Angelica in *Love for Love*? How will Ann Whitefield catch Jack Tanner in *Man and Superman*?). This imitation of some continuous and interesting action allows us to go right back to Aristotle if we wish without too much difficulty. Such a structuring is even more easy to trace in Ibsen's realistic plays, I think. Fergusson's description of *Ghosts*[2] is only the best known of the critical attacks on Ibsen's Scribean paraphernalia and his inability to quite shake it.[3] Only Chekhov

[1] I think this tendency in Shaw to wrap it up in a wedding dance is much less obvious than in someone like Wilde, where the echo is really strong. Here is the end of *The Importance of Being Earnest:*

JACK   My own one!
CHASABLE [*to Miss Prim*]   Laetitia! [*He embraces her.*]
MISS PRIM [*enthusiastically*]   Frederick! At last!
ALGERNON   Cecily! [*He embraces her.*] At last!
JACK   Gwendolen! [*He embraces her.*] At last!
LADY BRACKNELL   My nephew, you seem to be displaying signs of triviality.
JACK   On the contrary, Aunt Augusta, I've now realized for the first time in my life the vital Importance of Being Earnest.

Everything is there but the music!

[2] Francis Fergusson, in his book *Idea of a Theatre* (Princeton University Press, 1949), is interesting on both Ibsen and Chekhov, particularly on their structure. His judgment of *Ghosts*, though I am not in total agreement, suggests the Scribean overlay on the play which I do think is there: "At the end of the play the tragic rhythm of Mrs. Alving's quest is not so much completed as brutally truncated, in obedience to the requirements of the thesis and thriller. Oswald's collapse, before our eyes, with his mother's screaming, makes the intrigue end with a bang, and hammers home the thesis. But from the point of view of Mrs. Alving's tragic quest as we have seen it develop through the rest of the play, this conclusion concludes nothing: it is merely sensational."
Fergusson's value is his recognition of the importance of plots in plays. I think he sometimes simplifies—I think he is particularly guilty in his reading of both Ibsen and Chekhov, but the Scribean echoes in *Ghosts* and *Hedda Gabler* are certainly a difficulty in the plays.

[3] I do not include *Peer Gynt* or *Brand* here or even *The Master Builder* and *When We Dead Awaken*. Neither of the first two suggests, either in language or in structure, the kind of realism toward which I think the theatre was headed in the nineteenth century. Like *Faust*, they are unique national monuments worth a book in themselves. As for the last two, I am as yet in my reading of them simply confused. I don't know Norwegian, but in translation it is hard to be sure of the tone of the two plays. Are they laughing at the realistic structure

creates a new form, and interestingly enough an inimitable one. No one has really tried unless one believes Shaw's claim for *Heartbreak House*, a claim I find delightfully Shavian and altogether untrue.

As I have suggested above, drama traditionally has lent itself to analysis by the careful phrasing of its central action. This action in most plays is explicit and can be phrased in some kind of question. (It is this fact that suggests our continuing interest in Aristotle's *Poetics*, I think.) Who killed Laius? What will a man do to an uncle who has whored his mother and murdered his father? Will Mirabell be able to marry Millamant (which question includes getting the money from Lady Wishfort that might support such a marriage)? Has Mrs. Alving learned enough about the "joy of life" to know what to do when her son goes mad? The questions as here given may be overly simple, but they describe a way of understanding the plays to which they relate. The way they are phrased may well determine the way we see the play. One may talk about *Hamlet* in terms of "Will Claudius give himself away?" or in terms of "What keeps Hamlet from taking action?" But the questions and the actions in the play that answer them are a way to describe what happens in the play and at the same time describe what the play is about.

All of the talk that takes place between Mrs. Alving, Manders, Oswald, and Regina on the fatal evening before Oswald's disease catches up with him—the orphanage as a monument to her husband, Regina's giggles in the back room, the burning of the orphanage, the books on Mrs. Alving's bookshelf that so shock Manders—are all part of Mrs. Alving's discovery of what she is and what she might be. Everything in the play leads to the new crisis in which her new sense of herself will be put to the test. Ibsen shapes everything toward that end. Such shaping toward the resolution of some explicable problem is seemingly typical of drama before Chekhov, and much of that which has followed him. It does not, however, at least in this form, satisfactorily describe what happens in Chekhov himself, at least not in my reading.

---

they are couched in? Do they laugh at the central figures they deal with? Are Solness or Hilde or Irene to be taken as flesh and blood or as allegory? And in either case, taken how? It is as if in both these plays Ibsen is looking for some way to escape the realistic structure that has imprisoned him for forty years, but at present I simply don't know.

Let me look with some attention at *The Three Sisters* to see just what does happen. It is, first of all, difficult to find any problem posed or solved, and because of this it is difficult, at first, to see any action at all. When one looks at the problem the other way—that is, when one looks for the action first, forgetting about whether it answers any questions—one is perhaps surprised to discover a great number of actions. The most obviously unifying action is the departure of the army, after the five or so years the play occupies.[4] Their departure is not unlike the selling of the cherry orchard in the play of that name. In other words, the social world that occupies both plays leaves. The three sisters are the daughters of an army colonel; their life is socially defined by the army. They are as much of that class as Madame Ranavskaya is of hers, and the departure of the army in this play means much the same thing as Madame Ranavskaya's departure from her cherry orchard does.

Certainly the army's arrival for Irena's saint's day (the party is the action of the first act of the play) in the persons of Toozenbach, Solyony, Chebutykin, and Vershinnin defines the world in which the three sisters operate. Even though Masha is married to the school teacher Kulygin, it is her affair with Vershinnin that occupies us and her throughout the play. And in the largest sense the army leaves at the end of the play, and this departure might suggest a structural action for the whole play. This action, however, no more tells us what the play is about than does an analysis of the action of each act.

The first act is the celebration of Irena's saint's day, the second is an abortive attempt to celebrate a carnival party, the third is the attempt of the sisters to get some sleep after fighting a fire, and the fourth is their farewells to the army as it marches away in the distance. In Aristotelian terms, these are the actions imitated. None of these actions defines the meaning of the play, and yet the climax

[4] I don't think one can be very certain about the length of time the play encompasses. In the last act, Toozenbach says it is five years since he first began to love Irena, and I suppose we could assume the love started at her saint's day, but it is hardly definitive. The other hint concerning time is reflected in Natasha and Andrey's two children, one of whom is beginning to talk in the last act. But since the two weren't married in the first act, one can only be sure of two or three years of child raising. And finally, Chebutykin says in Act I that he is almost sixty, and in Act IV that he will retire from the army in a year. Time has passed, but Chekhov seems uninterested in letting us know how much with any exactness.

of each act resolves those actions. In the first, the photographs taken by Fedotik and Rodé of the celebrants at Irena's saint's day at dinner—their wish for many happy returns—climax, indeed freeze for us, the strangely unexciting party. In the second, the climax is Natasha's interruption of a possible party during carnival week because it might disturb her apparently sick child. The third act climaxes in Andrey's confession, the last of a series of despairing confessions—Irena's, Olga's, and Masha's having preceded it. And though these actions may seem unrelated to the rest of their respective acts, they are, in fact, the natural resolution to the kind of action that they succeed. In the second act, for example, Natasha's interruption of the kind of connection that a party suggests is the last in a series of such interruptions. The act opens with Natasha suggesting this possibility in her conversation with Andrey as she tells him about Bobik's being cold. Natasha, the outsider in Act I, is pretty clearly a force in Act II. She hints here not only at the termination of the party but also at the removal of Olga to Irena's room (the condition of the third act), and we are gradually being prepared for her removal from the house of everyone, which is the condition we are made aware of, in fact that we see, in the fourth act.

To look simply at these actions does not, I think, define the play for us, but they do have in common the difficulty all of the characters have in coming to terms with anything. There is something grotesquely inadequate about that first-act photograph as a record of the kind of joy and oneness we like to think typical of a birthday party. It is perhaps a fitting remembrance of the disconnected celebration we have seen. So, too, Natasha's interruption of the carnival stops what seems to be culminating in the joyful togetherness of a good party. In the third act, even the comfort and relief from irritation that sleep can bring are denied the sisters, and the play closes with the series of permanent farewells, with no hope of any of those parting meeting again, of even being able to attempt connection. If connection with one another and ease with themselves are difficult for the sisters and Andrey, they are not for Natasha. Ease for her is to get things done the way she wishes; connection is to make people do them. She accomplishes both with no difficulty. Compare the liaison she establishes with the never seen Protopopov to the comparable affair of Masha and Vershinnin.

How satisfactory the former! How complicated, how uncomfortable, even in such a very human way how foolish, the latter! Natasha may be crude and insensitive; certainly she is less sympathetic than the Prozorovs. But since her desires are achievable, she is certainly a more contented creature than anyone else in the play. The sensibilities of the Prozorov family make any kind of accomplishment difficult. As Olga says to Natasha concerning her rudeness to Anfisa in Act III, "It may be that we've been brought up in a peculiar way, but anyway I just can't bear it. When people are treated like that, it gets me down, I feel quite ill . . ."[5] Certainly Natasha has no such feeling, and her success in getting to her own particular Moscow is in pointed contrast to the sisters' inability to reach theirs.

Perhaps this problem of connection and Chekhov's way of showing it is most easily demonstrated in the second act. The first attempt at connection is made by Andrey in his talk with Ferapont. It is a ridiculous attempt at connection since Andrey unburdens himself to Ferapont precisely because he is too deaf to hear him. The release explicit in his disgust with himself because he is not a professor, because he is only a secretary to the local educational council, is possible only because it is to no one who can hear or respond to him. As he says to Ferapont's apology for not being able to hear:

If you could hear properly I don't think I'd be talking to you like this. I must talk to someone, but my wife doesn't seem to understand me, and as for my sisters . . . I'm afraid of them for some reason or other, I'm afraid of them laughing at me and pulling my leg . . . [Act II]

It is a one-sided conversation that is helpful to Andrey only because no one has heard it.

The next conversation starts out more hopefully. It is Vershinin's declaration of love to Masha, a declaration that thrills her and also embarrasses her:

When you talk to me like that, somehow I can't help laughing, although I'm afraid at the same time. Don't say it again, please. [Half-audibly] Well, no . . . go on. I don't mind . . . [Covers her face with her hands.] I don't mind . . . Someone's coming . . . Let's talk about something else. [Act II]

5 All quotations from Chekhov's plays are taken from Elizaveta Fen's translations as they appear in the Penguin Classics Series, Penguin Books, Baltimore, Maryland.

The natural result of Vershinnin's declaration should be some kind of decision for Masha to accept or reject. Certainly the interruption at this point by Toozenbach and Irena is not a disastrous one. It gives Masha time to think, time to collect herself. But before that possible collection and response can take place, Vershinnin is called away by his daughter—his "wife has taken poison again." The net result of the conversation is a frustrated inconclusiveness. Masha's immediate reaction is to get furious at Anfisa and then in turn at Irena and Chebutykin. The most obvious cause of her distress is that whatever had begun between herself and Vershinnin has been stopped, at least for the present cut off.[6] The important thing here is that the possible connection between them is short-circuited.

Irena and Toozenbach enter at this point, not angry with each other, but hardly hearing each other. Toozenbach tells her how he spends his life pursuing her (apparently unsuccessfully), and she answers (one is not sure to whom) that she is very tired. The disconnection, strangely enough, is not an unpleasant one. Irena is tired but relaxed, and Toozenbach, though hardly a successful lover, is not unhappy. When the doctor knocks from below, Irena says to Toozenbach: "Will you answer him, dear? . . . I can't. . . . I'm tired." And Toozenbach's compliance (he knocks on the floor) suggests at least a comfortable relationship. And that relationship, that sense of togetherness among the four of them—Vershinnin, Toozenbach, Masha, and Irena—centers on the doctor as he enters. The following exchange, though of no seeming importance, is one of these little moments of togetherness that Chekhov manages so unobtrusively, so almost unnoticeably:

[*Enter* CHEBUTYKIN. *He has been resting on his bed since dinner and has only just got up. He combs his beard, then sits down at the table and takes out a newspaper.*]

MASHA There he is. Has he paid his rent yet?
IRENA [*laughs*] No. Not a penny for the last eight months. I suppose he's forgotten. How solemn he looks sitting there!

---

6 It is never really clear from the play whether the affair is consummated. The closest thing to a hint is Masha's announcement in Act III that she loves Vershinnin, after which she leaves the room. Shortly after, Kulygin enters looking for her, and as far as we know he doesn't find her. Is she off with Vershinnin? Certainly the evidence is inconclusive enough to make us doubt the value or at least the connection most of us think of as part of the sexual act.

[*They all laugh. A pause.*]

I<small>RENA</small> Why don't you say something, Alexandr Ignatyevitch? [Act II]

In that pause before the next unit starts with Alexandr saying something, there is a moment of togetherness, a moment of what everyone hopes for in the party later. It is just a moment, it can't be held, it is perhaps not even fully understood; but it is there. The act moves on, trying to make the connection last, trying somehow to make it real, to talk about it. Alexandr's attempt immediately to start a discussion with Toozenbach for the benefit of all present, "a bit of philosophizing," is his reach toward connection, toward communication. What it shows is the inadequacy of words to make any such movement, to do anything except make words, make sounds. Perhaps the most pertinent thing about the moment of connection is the way it is expressed; indeed, it is the way most of Chekhov's moments that give us our reason for continued attempts at connection take place. It is not only casual, but accidental, terribly indirect. It takes place in the pause. Language can't manage it. Our focus is not on what is said, but on the fact that Masha and Irena, Toozenbach and Vershinnin, have seen the same thing the same way. It is this indirection that makes Chekhov so damnably difficult to stage; our usual theatrical devices are the wrong ones. That which points or heightens also destroys. To explain, to point out, is to lose what was there. It is what makes what Chekhov says so untheatrical.

The first act has a number of such moments, some sad, some happy; but their importance is that they happen and are somehow recognized by the people they happen to. It is not that verbal points are made or that major conflicts are resolved. Language is minor in this almost unconscious search for connection. The needs, or perhaps I should say the moments of connection, are much more basic than language.

Even when language seems important, it is after the fact. In Act I, for example, the sisters have been teasing Andrey after his initial appearance on stage. He finally makes them stop, and in his attempt to describe himself to Vershinnin, the newcomer, he manages to establish one of those moments of togetherness with his sisters. It is a moment of stasis, of frozen connection, of understanding that can't be discussed, that makes one think of a photograph. It is not, I think, accidental that the climax of Irena's saint's-day party is a photograph taken of the group. But let me quote the scene:

ANDREY   Yes. My father—God bless his memory—used to simply wear us out with learning. It sounds silly, I know, but I confess that since he died I've begun to grow stout, as if I'd been physically relieved of the strain. I've grown quite stout in a year. Yes, thanks to Father, my sisters and I know French and German and English, and Irena here knows Italian, too. But what an effort it all cost us!

MASHA   Knowing three languages in a town like this is an unnecessary luxury. In fact, not even a luxury, but just sort of useless encumbrance . . . it's rather like having a sixth finger on your hand. We know a lot of stuff that's useless.

VERSHININ   Really! [Laughs.] You know a lot of stuff that's useless! It seems to me that there's no place on earth, however dull and depressing it may be, where intelligence and education can be useless. Let us suppose that among the hundred thousand people in this town, all of them, no doubt, very backward and uncultured, there are just three people like yourselves. Obviously, you can't hope to triumph over all the mass of ignorance around you; as your life goes by, you'll have to keep giving in little by little until you get lost in the crowd, in the hundred thousand. Life will swallow you up, but you'll not quite disappear, you'll make some impression on it. After you've gone, perhaps six more people like you will turn up, then twelve, and so on, until in the end most people will have become like you. So in two or three hundred years life on this old earth of ours will have become marvellously beautiful. Man longs for a life like that, and if it isn't here yet, he must imagine it, wait for it, dream about it, prepare for it, he must know and see more than his father and his grandfather did. [Laughs.] And you're complaining because you know a lot of stuff that's useless.

MASHA [takes off her hat]   I'll be staying to lunch.

IRENA [with a sigh]   Really, someone should have written all that down.

[ANDREY has left the room unnoticed.]   [Act I]

To understand fully what I think happens in the quoted sequence, one must remember what has immediately preceded it. Andrey's sisters and the doctor have been teasing him because of his love for Natasha, and he has finally lost his temper and let us see his upset. He speaks of the difficulty he has sleeping, of his extended reading, and of his desire to translate a book into English. When Vershinnin says with some awe, "You read English then?" I think we must see the pride his sisters have in Andrey and their readiness to rush to his defense, to comfort and surround him, to understand the difficulties his talents and education must face in this backwater where they all live. Masha's understanding of his pain and, as she reads it, boredom, is, I think, echoed by Irena and Olga. The family focus of the sisters, despite their recent teasing of him, is on their brilliant brother. It is that moment of mutual pride among the sisters that I think forms the closest moment of connection in the unit I have quoted. It is not what is said, but what is felt around the words. Vershinnin's speech is a speech, all words about how people will get better and life will be beautiful, and yet it suggests less the possibility of connection than that moment which precedes it.

To be sure, the moment of connection between Andrey and his sisters comes in a kind of mutual depression just before Vershinnin's speech, a speech that is delivered, at least in part, to break that depression. What is interesting, however, is that the moment of connection between the brother and sisters is much more moving than the speech itself. True, Masha decides, after it is given, to stay to lunch, and Irena, apparently moved, suggests it should have been written down; but their responses, coupled with Andrey's departure during the speech, suggest not new connection as much as a depression which did connect and has been broken. Even if during the speech the girls are moved out of their depression, the new vision is less persuasive to us as a moment of connection than the moment that preceded it.

Words are so terribly inadequate in Chekhov. Whenever someone seems to be getting somewhere with them, they are somehow undercut. Perhaps the most persuasive moment in Chekhov is that strangely moving one in the second act of *The Cherry Orchard* when, after both Trofimov and Lopahin have spoken with some passion about what Russia is and what it might be, Liubov brings the conversation to earth by commenting on Lopahin's image of the Russians as giants, "Whatever do you want giants for? They're all right in fairy-tales, otherwise they're just terrifying." And then to point out what is really important, we have the stage directions [YEPIHODOV *crosses the stage in the background, playing his guitar.*] and Liubov's remark "There goes Yepihodov," echoed by Anya's "There goes Yepihodov." It is as if somehow all talk, all fiction, all imagination founder in any given human being, perhaps because we are all no more than two-and-twenty-mistakes Yepihodov. It is invariably the moment when one doesn't talk, when one can't, that catches us.

Again in the first act of *The Three Sisters* it is the embarrassing moment of no talk after Chebutykin's birthday present to Irena that we notice:

CHEBUTYKIN [*tearfully and crossly*] Expensive presents! . . . Get along with you! [*To the orderly*] Put the samovar over there. [*Mimics* IRENA.] Expensive presents! [Act I]

It is this moment of mutual embarrassment shared by Irena and Chebutykin and us that catches us, not the heartfelt explanation of why he did it that precedes this moment. In those rare moments when a speech seems to have been understood or seems to have defined something, consider what happens to it. Here is Masha's big speech just before her attempt at an exit in Act I; look what happens to it:

MASHA . . . Good-bye, my darling. [*Kisses* IRENA.] And once again—I wish you all the happiness in the world. In the old days when Father was alive we used to have thirty or forty officers at our parties. What gay parties we had! And today—what have we got today? A man and a half, and the place is as quiet as a tomb. I'm going home. I'm depressed today, I'm sad, so don't listen to me. [*Laughs through her tears.*] We'll have a talk later, but good-bye for now, my dear. I'll go somewhere or other . . .
IRENA [*displeased*] Really, you are a . . .
OLGA [*tearfully*] I understand you, Masha.
SOLYONY If a man starts philosophizing, you call that philosophy or possibly just sophistry, but if a woman or a couple of women start philosophizing you call that . . . what would you call that, now? Ask me another.
MASHA What are you talking about? You are a disconcerting person!
SOLYONY Nothing.

> 'He had no time to say "oh, oh!"
> Before the bear had struck him low' . . .

[*A pause.*]

MASHA [*to* OLGA *crossly*] Do stop snivelling! [Act I]

I think the speech is given as a truth for Masha that she would like the world to recognize as simple truth, a truth she would like to have had her listeners ponder so that she could leave in their remembrance a sense of her insight into life. Instead, Irena is pettishly disappointed and not at all interested in old times, Olga is sentimentally reminiscent, and Solyony (having been either the man or the half referred to) lets loose his carefully cultivated romantic temper. Masha looks with some dismay at the effect of her speech, tries to snap Olga out of her wrong view, still perhaps in hopes of an exit, only to be interrupted by the arrival of Anfisa and Ferapont. It completely undercuts her announcement, not unlike that moment in *The Cherry Orchard* when Lopahin returns to announce that he has bought the orchard only to be hit (or perhaps swung at) on the head by a pool cue.

Continually in the play there is near connection, but always concluding any given act it is the impossibility of making it that we are left with, and this is particularly true when speech is used. After that moment with the two sisters and their wooers in Act II as they look at the doctor, we have a long discussion between Toozenbach and Vershinnin, a discussion that even Masha joins, that is again an attempt to hold onto, to find ways to verbalize, that agreement that they had as they looked at Chebutykin. But as always, it peters out, the moment goes, it is never as strong as it is when it can't be talked about. Masha's concluding addition to the discussion is moving, but look what happens to it:

MASHA I think a human being has got to have some faith, or at least he's got to seek faith. Otherwise his life will be empty, empty. . . . How can you live and not know why the cranes fly, why children are born, why the stars shine in the sky! . . . You must either know why you live, or else . . . nothing matters . . . everything's just wild grass.

[*A pause.*]

VERSHINNIN All the same, I'm sorry my youth's over.
MASHA 'It's a bore to be alive in this world, friends,' that's what Gogol says.
TOOZENBACH And I feel like saying: it's hopeless arguing with you, friends! I give you up.
CHEBUTYKIN [*reads out of the paper*] Balzac's marriage took place at Berdichev.

[IRENA *sings softly to herself.*]

CHEBUTYKIN Must write this down in my notebook. [*Writes*] Balzac's marriage took place at Berdichev.   [Act II]

The need to make sense, to understand, is touchingly real, but Vershinnin's best response is a plea for his youth; Masha, herself, refutes herself; and Toozenbach stops the conversation. As if to put a capper on how *unfar* the conversation has carried us, Chebutykin's complete irrelevance makes its own comment on knowledge, on the search for knowledge. This is probably the most verbal attempt at communication in the play, but it is hardly successful.

In this act, Masha's connection with Vershinnin is destroyed by his exit to his suicidal wife, and finally Natasha's announcement that there can be no party ends all attempts at connection. The climax of the act—that is, the most moving attempt at some kind of connection—is Masha's dance to Toozenbach's piano, singing or shouting, "The Baron is drunk, the Baron is drunk." There is a desperate quality in this moment, but it hints at a possible connection at some basic level, almost like the rhythmic responses a group gives to a jazz artist. The waltz, the dance, the lines almost as words to a song suggest at least such a possibility. Natasha's interruption—an indirect interruption incidentally, carried not by Natasha's words but from her through Chebutykin—stops even this. Even the confrontation inherent in her opposition to their enjoyment is indirect. There is no "Please, this must stop," but a whisper to Ivan Romanych, after which she exits. Again there is nothing manageable enough to be focused through words. As always in Chekhov, the important moment comes somehow indirectly. One remembers Vanya's big attack on Serebrakov with the pistol, only to miss him. So here the celebration peters out. People gradually disperse, the carnival revelers are told off-stage to go home, we never hear them. Natasha passes through once more on her way to meet Protopopov for a drive—Bobik, though fitful, is of minor concern in the face of such an invitation—and the house is left to Irena, who *"alone with intense longing"* says, "Moscow! Moscow! Moscow!"—that cry for meaning in life somewhere.

The party which never comes off is not unlike, in miniature, the meaning of the whole play. We see a society that never comes off, that never relates in any definitive way which would allow us to call the society "social." There is no real connection in the four actions of the play, except that each act defines an event, and the way people react to that event allows us to see them. The important thing is not the meaning of the action itself, but the way people involved in the action respond to one another. The activities of each act allow us to listen to them. Like the impossibility of definable connection that the plays leave us with, so the structure of each is seemingly unpatterned. The traditional single action that has some resolution into meaning is purposely missing here, as if Chekhov knew that such resolutions in life are impossible. If art is to reflect life, it must reflect its fragmentation, its many actions that don't make sense, its chaos that we fitfully and usually unsatisfactorily try to pattern. The order in life is our imposition; the chaos is the natural state of things, and it is this futile but admirable attempt at making order, at making connection, that so touches us in Chekhov's plays. This way of patterning plays is true of each of the three last works of Chekhov. *The Cherry Orchard* is the tightest play of the three since everything is quite intimately and directly concerned with the sale of the orchard and with the consequences of the sale for those who live in the house. In *Uncle Vanya* the departure from the house of Serebrakov and Helena does not really become apparent until Serebrakov's announcement in Act III.[7]

I don't quite include *The Seagull* in this structuring because I think it is not as finished a work as the later pieces. Ibsen and direct confrontation with language still hang over it in crucial moments. The most crucial moment is Nina's attempt in the last act to explain herself. Later characters of Chekhov don't do this, either because they don't know themselves that well or because Chekhov recognizes the inadequacy of such explanation. His characters talk, often movingly—Trofimov in *The Cherry Orchard,* Astrov in *Uncle Vanya,* Vershinnin in *The Three Sisters*—but they talk about Russia or land conservation, not about their own particular problems. Even Vershinnin's talk about his family, his wife and children, is a standard subject for him, not an attempt at resolving or understanding his problems. Toozenbach introduces him as a man who

. . . calls on everybody and tells them that he's got a wife and two little girls. He'll tell you about it, too, I'm sure of that. His wife seems to be a bit soft in the head. She wears a long plait like a girl, she is always philosophizing and talking in high-flown language, and then she often tries to commit suicide, apparently just to annoy her husband. I would have run away from a wife like that years ago, but he puts up with it, and just grumbles about it.   [Act I]

7 The meaning of arrivals and departures in all of Chekhov's plays is discussed in the article by Arthur Ganz listed in the Bibliographical Essay.

With such an introduction, we can hardly take Vershinnin's talk about his family as personal crisis. Even Masha, who is to fall in love with him, describes him in comic terms:

. . . I thought he was queer at first, then I started to pity him . . . then I began to love him . . . love everything about him—his voice, his talk, his misfortunes, his two little girls. . . . [Act III]

There is finally something moving in Vershinnin, as in all of Chekhov's characters, but it is not his plight. One cares for him, as does Masha, despite his worry about his wife and children, which is almost comic. In Nina's case those last speeches are neither comically set up nor habitual. They are attempts to demonstrate, through speech, what her difficulties as a human being are. We see her, where we do not see later Chekhov characters, in emotional crisis. People don't live here; they don't have certain speeches, and Chekhov realizes it in his last plays. His practice there is to refuse to demonstrate character in such situations. But listen to Nina:

I am so tired. Oh, I wish I could rest . . . just rest! [*Raising her head*] I'm a seagull . . . No, that's not it. I'm an actress. Oh, well! [*She hears* ARKADINA *and* TRIGORIN *laughing off-stage, listens, then runs to the door at left and looks through the keyhole.*] So he is here, too! [*Returning to* TREPLIOV] Oh, well! . . . Never mind . . . Yes . . . He didn't believe in the theatre, he was always laughing at my dreams, and so gradually I ceased to believe, too, and lost heart . . . And then I was so preoccupied with love and jealousy, and a constant fear for my baby . . . I became petty and common, when I acted I did it stupidly . . . I didn't know what to do with my hands or how to stand on the stage, I couldn't control my voice . . . But you can't imagine what it feels like—when you know that you are acting abominably. I'm a seagull. No, that's not it again. . . . Do you remember you shot a seagull? A man came along by chance, saw it and destroyed it, just to pass the time . . . A subject for a short story . . . That's not it. [*Rubs her forehead.*] What was I talking about? [Act IV]

And so it continues. She goes on to describe the changes in her, in her acting, and so on. The point is that the speech is an attempt to depict something almost like a mental breakdown, a confession that is real, a meaningful moment in one's life, a turning point that can be demonstrated in pantomime and speech. Her desperation and confusion, caught in the constant references to the seagull and its relation to her, and her inability to remember what she is talking about are both attempts at a kind of realistic psychological portrait of a woman in a crisis in her life. It is a very hard speech to make convincing within the less theatrically climactic, more realistic context of the rest of the play, and Chekhov seems to have known it. He doesn't fall into that trap in later plays, and as a consequence his dramatic texture, though often very hard to describe and perhaps equally hard to realize in production, is of a piece. Of that, one is always keenly aware. It is, in fact, one of the most persuasive aspects of his plays. His use of language, unlike that of Ibsen and his predecessors, is not to demonstrate climactic moments, because life isn't built on climactic moments.

CHAPTER V

VI

Pinter: A Logical Continuation

It may seem strange to move from Chekhov to Pinter in a study of language in drama. In fact, it is strange to think of Chekhov in this regard. Certainly the drama of Eliot or Yeats or Fry suggests a concern with language that is a good deal more obvious than is that of either Chekhov or Pinter. Pinter, however, seems in the stream of drama—I suppose one must still call it the realistic stream—which dominates our theatres and most concerns our actors. There is something special about poetic dramatists that makes them suspect except in those rare cases where their method or concern is available to actors and indeed to other playwrights. Brecht, for example, a playwright I don't much care for, is an important playwright if for no other reason than his influence on actors—"alienation" is still a term that actors feel they must come to terms with—and on playwrights. I doubt very much that Osborne would have ever written *Luther* in quite the form he did without Brecht's examples of similar structure before him. Even Bolt's *A Man for All Seasons,* a thoroughly conventional play, seems to borrow the Common Man from the presentational aspect of Brechtian dramaturgy.

Pinter, unlike Fry and Eliot, much less Yeats, is working out of the realistic tradition. To get at his intentions, at least as I understand them, actors find themselves not only using the by now almost passé "method," but being asked to shift their point of attack much more quickly than normal psychology would allow and for much less valid reasons. In Chekhovian drama, for example, the kind of psychological realism in which Stanislavsky and his followers were most at home—the digging into a personal life of a character, the

117

examination of the events that have put a given character in the situation he or she is in, the insistence on putting one's own life into the character—is often a real help to the creation of the texture Chekhov gives us. In Pinter such concern is certainly helpful, but it is not enough. Too often, we cannot find the situation that surrounds a character, and our plumbing into his or her personal life only gives us guesses, often misleading and usually extraneous. I can, with some certainty, create a life for Masha in *The Three Sisters*. I know, after all, a good deal about her, her family, her upbringing, her hopes, her marriage, and the limitations of her husband. If I don't know for sure whether her passion for Vershinnin has been consummated, I do know why that passion is of such importance to her. I can understand the situation that led to her falling in love with him in such a way as to create a persuasive case for doing what she does.

This is not true in Pinter's plays. What do I really know about Rose in *The Room*? Where did she come from? What is her relation to the Negro? What kind of an apartment house (the size of which even the landlord is not sure) does she live in? Why does her contact with the Negro finally make her blind? It is true that answers to these questions may not be necessary for an actress to find in order to make the part work, but of equal importance is the fact that they are the kinds of questions that a method-oriented actor would ask of a part. So, too, Stanley in *The Birthday Party,* the two brothers in *The Caretaker,* and the two criminals in *The Dumbwaiter* are involved in situations that are never really clarified for us and about which we need not know to create Pinter's particular view of the human condition. Where tangible situations motivated Chekhov's characters, tone of voice motivates Pinter's. Where a real wife and two daughters frustrate Vershinnin's affair with Masha, not to mention Masha's very real husband, a gesture frustrates Rose, an illogical question frustrates Stanley. The thoroughness of the frustration in the two playwrights may be comparable; the causes of frustration seem to me quite different. Where Chekhov seems at pains to show characters trying to make language work, trying to communicate, Pinter seems at pains to show characters trying to hide behind language, almost unaware of its implications—or at the other extreme, completely aware that one can make it imply anything.

Pinter's own remarks on language in the London Sunday *Times* of March 4, 1962, are of particular interest in this regard:

Beware the writer who puts forward his concern for you to embrace. . . . This kind of writer clearly trusts words absolutely. I have mixed feelings about words myself. Moving among them, sorting them out, watching them appear on the page, from this I derive a considerable pleasure. But at the same time I have another strong feeling about words which amounts to nothing less than nausea. Such a weight of words confronts us, day in day out, . . . the bulk of it a stale dead terminology; ideas endlessly repeated and permutated, become platitudinous, trite, meaningless. Given this nausea, it's very easy to be overcome by it and step back into paralysis. . . . But if it is possible to confront this nausea, to follow it to its hilt and move through it, then it is possible to say something has occurred, that something has even been achieved.

Language, under these conditions, is a highly ambiguous commerce. So often, below the words spoken, is the thing known and unspoken. . . .

There are two silences. One when no word is spoken. The other when perhaps a torrent of language is being employed. This speech is speaking of a language locked beneath it. That is its continual reference. The speech we hear is an indication of that we don't hear. It is a necessary avoidance, a violent, sly, anguished or mocking smoke-screen which keeps the other in its place. When true silence falls we are still left with echo but are nearer nakedness. One way of looking at speech is to say it is a constant stratagem to cover nakedness.

. . . I think that we communicate only too well, in our silence, in what is unsaid, and that what takes place is continual evasion, desperate rearguard attempts to keep ourselves to ourselves. Communication is too alarming. To enter into someone else's life is too frightening. To disclose to others the poverty within us is too fearsome a possibility.

I'm not suggesting that no character in a play can ever say what he in fact means. Not at all. I have found that there invariably does come a moment when this happens, where he says something, perhaps which he has never said before. And where this happens, what he says is irrevocable, and can never be taken back.

There is another factor which I think has considerable bearing on the matter and that is the immense difficulty, if not the impossibility, of verifying the past. I don't mean merely years ago, but yesterday, this morning. . . . If one can speak of the difficulty of knowing what in fact took place yesterday one can I think treat the present in the same way. . . . A moment is sucked away and distorted, often even at the time of its birth. We will all interpret a common experience differently, though we prefer to subscribe to the view that there is a shared, common ground, a known ground. I think there's a shared common ground all right, but that it's more like a quicksand. . . .

The statement seems to me not only fascinating (and, I might add, terrifyingly true, as indeed is Pinter's drama when it works well), but indicative of what is, to me, finally the most important facet of his dramatic statement. Let me try to illustrate with *The Birthday Party*. If one is to talk about the meaning of that play in terms of its theme, in terms of what it seems to say, I think one can give a perfectly fair idea of the play. For example, Bernard Dukore has written:

The subjection of the artist by the pressures of conformity is the chief concern of *The Birthday Party*. In this play, Pinter paints a frightening picture of the individual pressured by the forces of society to the point wherein he loses his individuality and becomes a drugged member of the social machine.[1]

This is a fair statement of the meaning that one can extract from what happens in the play. Stanley's apparent flight from the world in Meg's rooming house is depicted in Act I; his attempt at confronting that world takes place in Act II; and his resultant collapse stemming from this confrontation occurs in Act III. What is not so apparent is what motivates the attempted escape, the attempted confrontation, and finally the very real collapse. Motivation, or rather *explicable* motivation (explicable reasons for what happens) is nowhere to be found. People are continually changing direction in Pinter. One moves from attack to defense, from affection to dislike, from invitation to rejection in a line, but nowhere within that line or within the action that precedes the line can one comfortably account for that change. The only reason we assume a change has taken place is that the tone of a conversation has changed. We can at best guess at the reason for its change.

Let me look, for a moment, at what I feel is the climax of Act I, the moment in which Stanley comes closest to revealing himself. Urged by Meg to play the piano again, he first puts her off in a series of obvious (in their tone) fabrications about a job on a round-the-world tour. Gradually, however, the tone changes and the fabrications, the attempts at covering truth, break down; and in the following speech, it seems to me, one hears a real person talking about a real pain and a real fear. Stanley is speaking of his concert at Lower Edmonton:

[1] Bernard Dukore, "The Theatre of Harold Pinter," *Tulane Drama Review* (March, 1962), pp. 43–55.

CHAPTER VI

I had a unique touch. Absolutely unique. They came up to me. They came up to me and said they were grateful. Champagne we had that night, the lot. [*Pause.*] My father nearly came down to hear me. Well, I dropped him a card anyway. But I don't think he could make it. No, I—I lost the address, that was it. [*Pause.*] Yes. Lower Edmonton. Then after that, you know what they did? They carved me up. Carved me up. It was all arranged, it was all worked out. My next concert. Somewhere else it was. In winter. I went down there to play. Then, when I got there, the hall was closed, the place was shuttered up, not even a caretaker. They'd locked it up. [*Takes off his glasses and wipes them on his pyjama jacket.*] A fast one. They pulled a fast one. I'd like to know who was responsible for that. [*Bitterly*] All right, Jack, I can take a tip. They want me to crawl down on my bended knees. Well I can take a tip . . . any day of the week. [*He replaces his glasses, then looks at* MEG.] Look at her. You're just an old piece of rock cake, aren't you? [*He rises and leans across the table to her.*] That's what you are, aren't you? [Act I]²

Considering what immediately precedes the speech, I don't think a particularly good case can be made for the actuality of Stanley's unique touch, the critic's approval, or even the champagne. I am more persuaded of the actuality of a father, a father, furthermore, who is important to Stanley. That, I take it, is why it is so hard for him to verbalize why he wasn't at the concert. The very repetitions of inadequate explanations make the moment in the speech clearly important to Stanley and therefore, in my attempt to understand what is happening to him, important to me. I am again suspicious as he returns to the concert at Lower Edmonton; but when he suddenly speaks of being carved up, one assumes by the critics, and goes on to say that they want him down on bended knees, I do believe he is talking about a putdown, perhaps about his piano playing, perhaps about life in general. In fact, so exposed is he at this moment that he can turn to the Meg he has spent the act mocking and see her as a possible source of strength and comfort in that "You're just an old piece of rock cake, aren't you?" Something in the Edmonton concert experience, in which he felt deserted by his father and attacked by some impersonal "they"—whether critics in particular or the world at large—was important to him. The reference to his father is speech "speaking of a language locked beneath it. . . . an indication of [speech] we don't hear."

² All quotations are from the Grove Press edition of *The Birthday Party* and *The Room*, two plays in one volume.

Although what happened to Stanley is purposely left vague, I am persuaded that he is convinced he has been cut down and he needs support, strength. I am also convinced, having heard Meg's inability to understand anything, even to understand the meaning of "succulent," that Meg can't give it to him, even though for a moment he is hopeful. In my own reading, I even think his recognition of her inability to understand him underlies the next sequence in the play, in which he tells her (as one would tell a four-year-old about the big bad wolf) of a mysterious "they," wheeling a more mysterious wheelbarrow up the front path in their search for an again mysterious someone. He tells her, though in the form of a fairy tale, his own fears, his concern that someone will come and wheel him away.

In a sequence like this, I am not ready to defend an explicable event that causes Stanley's fears. I think Pinter's point is precisely one's inability—he is Kafkaesque in this—to explain. We are as much persuaded by sound as by actuality. Truth is not merely nebulous; it may indeed be nonexistent. Of course, Stanley, like many of us, can't accept this; he will understand, or at least be able to point out to all of us, that truth, a real relationship between people, exists, even if it must continually be distorted by the inanities and insensitivities of people like Meg. I have said that he points this conviction out to us, and this is too strong a description of what he does. It is, however, one way to explain his continued needling of Meg, his inability to really ignore her. He recognizes both the need and the difficulty of making her understand him. It is his need that makes me think he believes in the possibility. I think both elements, the need and the recognition of the difficulty in fulfilling that need, are present in the following exchange:

STANLEY [*quietly*]   Who do you think you're talking to?
MEG [*uncertainly*]   What?
STANLEY   Come here.
MEG   What do you mean?
STANLEY   Come over here.
MEG   No.
STANLEY   I want to ask you something.

[MEG *fidgets nervously. She does not go to him.*]

Come on. [*Pause.*] All right. I can ask it from here just as well. [*Deliberately*] Tell me, Mrs. Boles, when you address yourself to me, do you ever

ask yourself who exactly you are talking to? Eh? [*Silence. He groans, his trunk falls forward, his head falls into his hands.*]
MEG [*in a small voice*] Didn't you enjoy your breakfast, Stan? [Act I]

The need is certainly present in his insistent demand that Meg recognize who he is, ask herself "who exactly [she] is talking to"; the recognition of the difficulty, perhaps impossibility, of fulfilling that need is clear in the stage direction pointing out his collapse; and finally the reason for the difficulty is painfully clear in Meg's response, as if all could be explained by his eating habits. I suppose her inability to hear Stanley is most painfully felt in her response to his moving description about his attempts to give a concert, her "Did you pay a visit this morning, Stan?"

I don't think Stanley, and as a consequence the audience, can comfortably accept the fact that truth, logic, value, human connection may indeed be nothing but what people accept, no matter how meaningless, how illogical, or how valueless. Goldberg may know that truth is what people accept. As he says of McCann's nervousness, "It is more than true, it is a fact." Goldberg seems to know this; Stanley still only fears it. Goldberg can live there; Stanley cannot. Stanley will finally break. Goldberg will come close, but when in Act III his clichés of self-definition, of explanations of his position—"Follow the line, McCann"; "Play up, and play the game"; "Honour thy father and thy mother"; "learn by heart"— break down, he is not destroyed. Certainly he comes close:

Because I believe that the world . . . [*Vacant.*] . . .
Because I believe that the world . . . [*Desperate.*] . . .
BECAUSE I BELIEVE THAT THE WORLD . . . [*Lost.*] . . . [Act III]

But unlike Stanley, who a little later can sound his self-definition only in "Uh-gug . . . ug-gug . . . eeehhh-gag" and collapse, Goldberg will pull himself up by a new set of equally meaningless but more emotionally laden clichés. After that last "BECAUSE I BELIEVE THAT THE WORLD," he calls McCann to him and says:

[*Intensely, with growing certainty*] My father said to me, Benny, Benny, he said, come here. He was dying. I knelt down. By him day and night. Who else was there? Forgive, Benny, he said, and let live. Yes, Dad. Go home to your wife. I will, Dad. Keep an eye open for low-lives, for schnorrers and for layabouts. He didn't mention names. I lost my life in the service of others, he said, I'm not ashamed. Do your duty and keep your observations. Always bid good morning to the neighbours. Never, never, forget your family, for they are the rock, the constitution and the core! If you're ever in any difficulties Uncle Barney will see you in the clear. I knelt down. [*He kneels, facing* McCann.] I swore on the good book. And I knew the word I had to remember—Respect! Because McCann—[*Gently*] Seamus—who came before your father? His father. And who came before him? Before him? . . . [*Vacant—triumphant*] Who came before your father's father but your father's father's mother! Your great-gran-granny. [*Silence. He slowly rises.*] And that's why I've reached my position, McCann. [Act III]

It is a beautiful example of how language can cover, can protect, can hide. That moment of nakedness, of emptiness about what he believes the world to be, is here covered and the man recovered, not by truths, by words that mean anything, by a prose that cuts into what we are, but by emotionally laden platitudes about respect, about family, about Benny (the third name he has called himself— what do words mean?), about the good book (Why does it sound so like a bible for this Jew?), and finally about that almost Ionesco-like "great-gran-granny." He lives in a world of cover, of noise, of convention that he can manipulate toward his "position." I think one misses Goldberg if there isn't something pathetic, even moving, in his attempt to persuade himself. I hope indeed the attempt scares us a little.

In neither Stanley's concern in the first act nor Goldberg's in the third, can we account for these outbursts. Stanley is reminded of his life by his piano somehow (we can make up a story, but Pinter doesn't give us one), and Goldberg feels "knocked out" (again, we can make up reasons for his fatigue—the problems of breaking Stanley, of handling an irritated McCann, of misleading a suspicious Petey), but Pinter doesn't press the point or assure us of it. The events that might explain what we hear are not given us—only the tone. It is as if Pinter were saying that we are as much moved by manner, by what we hear, as by the substance or the reason for that manner. And throughout the play it is that manner, shifting without explicable reason, which taunts us, scares us, makes us laugh, and sometimes makes us shudder.

At the beginning of Act II, in the scene between McCann and Stanley, Pinter even takes us a step further. He gives us causes for change of tone, causes that are completely concrete and completely ridiculous. If in Act I the reasons for Stanley's shifts of attack on

CHAPTER VI

Meg were either vague or inexplicable, in Act II they are at first not at all vague, but even less explicable. The act opens with McCann seated, tearing a newspaper into strips, an action that has no meaning except its apparent importance to McCann, who concentrates on it with careful attention. Interestingly enough, the action also serves, for no explicable reason, as a stop to Stanley, who enters from the left, sees McCann and his paper, crosses the stage to the right in order to get a glass of water in the kitchen, and then returns to leave the room by the left exit. If one assumes that Stanley's main concern is leaving the house, the only reason for his staying would seem to center on his fascination with McCann's paper-tearing. The stage directions say that he watches McCann, and in the playing of the scene, regardless of how intensely one plays that interest, it is a fascination with the strange event that keeps Stanley temporarily in the room. To be sure, he breaks out of the spell in his attempt to exit from the kitchen across stage to the door on the other side, and he is intercepted by McCann on the way. The paper-tearing, however, has hypnotized Stanley into the room and allowed McCann to block his exit. It is not really imporant whether Stanley would ever leave the room or not—some readers, for example, insist that he couldn't under any circumstances. The point is that the paper-tearing acts on an audience as the immediate cause of Stanley's staying in the room rather than leaving, his apparent real intention from his first entrance in the act.

It is like a game of some kind, a game that McCann plays to lure his fly into the web. Once Stanley is there, the game changes. Stanley is now aware of some kind of trap, at least of some obstacle to his leaving and he faces it—faces it and, temporarily at least, removes it—in, of all things, a whistling contest:

McCANN   But they're holding a party here for you tonight.
STANLEY   Oh really? That's unfortunate.
McCANN   Ah no. It's very nice.

[*Voices from outside the back door.*]

STANLEY   I'm sorry. I'm not in the mood for a party tonight.
McCANN   Oh, is that so? I'm sorry.
STANLEY   Yes, I'm going out to celebrate quietly, on my own.
McCANN   That's a shame.

[*They stand.*]

STANLEY   Well, if you'd move out of my way—
McCANN   But everything's laid on. The guests are expected.
STANLEY   Guests? What guests?
McCANN   Myself for one. I had the honour of an invitation. [McCANN
begins to whistle "The Mountains of Morne."]
STANLEY [moving away]   I wouldn't call it an honour, would you? It'll
just be another booze-up.

[STANLEY joins McCANN in whistling "The Mountains of Morne." During
the next five lines the whistling is continuous, one whistling while the
other speaks, and both whistling together.]

McCANN   But it is an honour.
STANLEY   I'd say you were exaggerating.
McCANN   Oh no. I'd say it was an honour.
STANLEY   I'd say that was plain stupid.
McCANN   Oh no.

[They stare at each other.]

STANLEY   Who are the other guests?
McCANN   A young lady.
STANLEY   Oh yes? And . . . ?
McCANN   My friend.
STANLEY   Your friend?
McCANN   That's right. It's all laid on.

[STANLEY walks round the table towards the door. McCANN meets him.]

STANLEY   Excuse me.   [Act II]

I don't know "The Mountains of Morne," but I assume it starts as a
kind of mock of Stanley's weakness and a kind of banner of Mc-
Cann's authority. It might seem more relevant if the tune were
"Happy Birthday." At any rate, it serves as a gauntlet thrown at
Stanley, which he picks up, and the ensuing whistling at each
other is a duel—a duel which Stanley wins. He wins, if for no
other reason than that McCann stops the whistling which he, not
Stanley, started. And now, as if because he had won that round,
Stanley is able to question McCann. To be sure, he tries one more
escape, but when McCann admits openly that he will stop him,
rather than the indirect means of stopping him by pretending an
interest in Stanley's birthday, Stanley has won a point. McCann has
been forced to show his hand.

I think this forcing toward open confrontation is central not only
to this act, but to the whole character of Stanley. He is surrounded

by a world that will not talk straight, much less openly. In Act I, he has shown us repeatedly his disgust with Meg's vagueness, her inability to hear. No matter what kind of horror he calls her, she returns for more. If she asks politely how the corn flakes are, his reply, "Horrible," has no visible effect on her except to engage her in a defense which is more to make conversation than really to defend herself against the attack. She doesn't even flinch. Nor is she seriously bothered in the later attacks when Stanley calls her a bad wife who won't make her husband a cup of tea, who gives him bad milk instead. Her responses are conventional and suggest petulant annoyance rather than the kind of shock one might expect if she heard any of the remarks as real. Meg doesn't hear. One has the feeling Stanley could say anything to her, and it would make absolutely no difference. Indeed he tries, and the closest he gets to a response of shock is in her total misunderstanding of the word "succulent," a word she takes to mean something dirty. Her responses continually suggest her insensitivity to what goes on around her, and though that insensitivity annoys Stanley, it also protects him. As long as he tests himself against the likes of Meg, he can hold onto his convictions that the world would make sense but for the Megs in it. He can, in this womblike boarding house, curse at people's insensitivity without ever having to ask the truly basic question of whether it's their insensitivity to truth or that truth simply doesn't exist. In other words, Stanley can still believe that there are in the world other souls as sensitive as he is, committed as he is to the belief that somehow the world makes sense, that truth exists, as long as he can explain to himself that the reason one sees so little of this commitment is because most people are as stupid as Meg, as blind as Meg.

In Act II, in his confrontation with McCann, Stanley has a new sounding board, a new challenge. If he believes, as I think he does, that there is a way of facing life's problems directly because such problems are real and definable, then McCann's indirection, his pretence at friendship when he really means something else, can be broken down, can demonstrate for Stanley that the world is not pretence but real. In this whole sequence, he pursues McCann in an attempt to pin him, to make him openly admit why he is here, and what his real relation to Stanley is. The contest ends in a draw. McCann has not been able to break Stanley with his unsupported tone of threat, but Stanley has not been able to make McCann admit that the threat is unsupported, that there is no real reason why the two of them couldn't be friends, why indeed the whole thing hasn't been a game. "What about coming out to have a drink with me? There's a pub down the road serves draught Guinness. Very difficult to get in these parts—" But the appeal is broken off by Goldberg's nicely clichéd entrance line, "A mother in a million." The contest is a strange draw.

What is interesting is the number of directions the contest has taken. After the whistling sequence, Stanley has started his questioning of McCann ("So you're down here on holiday?") in an attempt to suggest that they may have met one another before, may indeed know each other. The push on McCann gets Stanley nowhere, and under the pressure of a simple questioning "Yes?" by McCann in response to an explanation by Stanley of where he has lived in Maidenhead, Stanley is forced to defend himself. The following sequence is one of those strange moments in Pinter when the whole burden of attack has shifted completely—one knows it by the tone of voice—but for no more reason than something in that tone of voice, in McCann's apparently innocent question. It is because of Stanley's near stuttering replies to explain how he got here that we are certain he is being attacked, even though we are not certain of what in McCann's question triggered the response. Somehow he has gotten to Stanley, and in a broken speech in which words don't quite suffice to cover his fears, Stanley tries to extricate himself from some trap he feels he is in. When McCann asks Stanley if he likes it here, Stanley replies:

Me? No. But you will. [*He sits at the table.*] I like it here, but I'll be moving soon. Back home. I'll stay there too, this time. No place like home. [*He laughs.*] I wouldn't have left, but business calls. Business called, and I had to leave for a bit. You know how it is.   [Act II]

It may be difficult to understand, but one certainly hears the uncertainty of a hurriedly thought-up defense. The cliché that embarrasses him, "No place like home," the repetition "business calls. Business called, and I had to leave for a bit," the appeal for help because of his own lack of clarity in "You know how it is" all suggest a Stanley backing up rather than pursuing. He is trying to answer questions now; he is no longer asking them. His unsureness and fear continue as he retreats without getting answers and McCann pursues without giving any. Stanley is again on the run.

Again, however, the tables turn. In a desperate lunge at straight talk, Stanley finally says:

STANLEY Listen. You knew what I was talking about before, didn't you?

McCANN I don't know what you're at at all.

STANLEY It's a mistake! Do you understand?

McCANN You're in a bad state, man.

STANLEY [*whispering, advancing*] Has he told you anything? Do you know what you're here for? Tell me. You needn't be frightened of me. Or hasn't he told you?

McCANN Told me what?

STANLEY [*hissing*] I've explained to you, damn you, that all those years I lived in Basingstoke I never stepped outside the door.

McCANN You know, I'm flabbergasted with you.

STANLEY [*reasonably*] Look. You look an honest man. You're being made a fool of, that's all. You understand? Where do you come from?

McCANN Where do you think?

STANLEY I know Ireland very well. I've many friends there. I love that country and I admire and trust its people. I trust them. They respect the truth and they have a sense of humour. I think their policemen are wonderful. I've been there. I've never seen such sunsets. What about coming out to have a drink with me? There's a pub down the road serves draught Guinness. Very difficult to get in these parts— [Act II]

And somehow in here, McCann begins to question himself, to look less sure, to give Stanley the opening he needs to pursue McCann rather than run from him. My own reading suggests it starts when Stanley says, "Or hasn't he told you?" I think I take that moment as a turn because of McCann's earlier conversation with Goldberg when he had pressed Nat hard for information about what the job here was and got no answer. Even though McCann seems to recover in "You know, I'm flabbergasted with you," Stanley's next speech suggests that the recovery doesn't really work. And in Pinter's world, a world where intonation is perhaps as much truth as we ever get, that is all the hint of change we are given. Stanley's sense that he has touched something pursuable is enough to give him at least the confidence to face Goldberg. If he has not made McCann admit an explicable reason for his attack, he has nevertheless seen in McCann's confusion the possibility that one could exist. Words still seem possible as a means of communication. One can talk, so Stanley still believes, with the possibility of communication taking place, with the possibility of both gaining information and making human contact. Indeed, the ensuing scene with Goldberg, Stanley, and McCann will test this belief.

The first crucial showdown in this confrontation, between Stanley's hope for an explicable world and Goldberg's conviction (whether realized or instinctive) that the world is what one makes it, is in what I call the first inquisition scene. It begins when, after Stanley's show of bravado in whistling off Goldberg's command to sit down, he decides to do it anyhow, seemingly on his own terms, seemingly sure of his ground. His first response to Goldberg's attack, to Goldberg's blast of questions, is to try to understand them. His responses, however, are also questions, simple questions of puzzlement:

GOLDBERG Webber, what were you doing yesterday?
STANLEY Yesterday?
GOLDBERG And the day before. What did you do the day before that?
STANLEY What do you mean?
GOLDBERG Why are you wasting everybody's time, Webber? Why are you getting in everybody's way?
STANLEY Me? What are you—
GOLDBERG I'm telling you, Webber. You're a washout. Why are you getting on everybody's wick? Why are you driving that old lady off her conk?
McCANN He likes to do it!
GOLDBERG Why do you behave so badly, Webber? Why do you force that old man out to play chess?
STANLEY Me?
GOLDBERG Why do you treat that young lady like a leper? She's not the leper, Webber!
STANLEY What the— [Act II]

The questions are undoubtedly unexpected in the vehemence of their attack, but they all refer to real possibilities. Stanley's getting in everybody's way was already suggested by Lulu in Act I. It is true that Stanley's indirect attacks on Meg might be construed as attempts to drive her crazy, just as it is true that Petey has gone to play chess and Stan has treated Lulu unchivalrously, at least in his first encounter with her. One might wonder how Goldberg knows all this, but a rational Stanley or a trying-to-believe-in-rational-discourse Stanley can hear the questions as having some reference to a reality he knows. The next sequence, with its series of near non-sequitur questions, is less easy to answer, and Stanley tries to dismiss them as meaningless ("You're on the wrong horse"), as answerable when relevant ("When did you come to this place?" "Last year."), as laughable when too personal ("Why did you come here?" "My feet hurt."), or as a joke gone too far when they pick him up on his tone ("Did you stir properly? Did they fizz?" "Now, now, wait, you—").

This last confusion, however, puts Stanley on a kind of defensive that he never can quite shake. After McCann and Goldberg have taken off his glasses, their questions become almost judicial, like a judge's in court, and though Stanley will still try to laugh them off, the laughs are harder to come by. The last exchange in this unit— his response of "Joe Soap" to "What's your name?"—leads to a series of questions about external authority, not now judicial authority but divine authority, that leads finally to his complete collapse. He may have been able to laugh off the seeming irrelevancy of what his name is, and he could answer perhaps flippy as to when he last washed a cup; but he cannot deal so easily with equally meaningless but to him apparently more important questions of what he believes in. It is after Goldberg's unanswered question "When did you last pray?" that McCann says, in what is apparently a sound observation, "He's sweating." The problems of prayer, of possibility, of necessity are important questions to Stanley. Although he cannot answer them in such a context, perhaps in any context, he cannot dismiss them; and once he has admitted the possibility of answering any question, he is of course at Goldberg's and McCann's mercy. Goldberg can, after all, ask anything about anything since he believes in nothing; Stanley is at his mercy because he would like to believe in something. It is as if Goldberg, aware that Stanley wants to believe, knows he can shove anything at him to show him how foolish he is in his desire, even "Which came first, the chicken or the egg?"—a repeated question that finally pushes Stanley to his first breakdown, a scream.

It is not that Stanley has given up on communication, only on words. He can still have convictions, as his kick of Goldberg and his attempted murder of Meg and rape of Lulu (if it is a rape) attest. What he can no longer do is talk. Talk, with all the limitations Pinter sees in it, is now in the hands of the party celebrants, Stanley's well-wishers. And what a vicious, ironic comment the phoney, confused congratulatory speeches make on the "birthday

party"—a kind of ritual deathday party, with the lovemaking of
Goldberg and Lulu on one side of the stage simply an echo of the
emptiness of Meg's and McCann's nostalgic, lonely reveries on the
other. There is no real celebration here, only the forms—the toasts,
the embraces, the singing, the drinking—empty of any meaning.
Only the game, blindman's buff, has any meaning, a kind of reverse
reflection of what games are supposed to be, culminating here not
in the comic delight of discovering that one's fear, one's giggling
worry that he might be caught, is groundless, but in the attempted
murder of Meg and rape of Lulu. What should end in "Whom will
he catch?" becomes "Whom will he kill?" Stanley may no longer be
able to speak about what he believes in, but he can still act upon it.
It is as if his attempted murder of Meg is an attempt to kill the
vague, unhearing attitude that so annoyed him in Act I; just as the
rape of Lulu must in some way be his own response to Goldberg's
lovemaking, an attempt to fight back, to prove that his own convictions are worth more than Goldberg's belief in nothing.

Act III returns to the same look at the world with which the play
opened. Petey and Meg are at breakfast—Petey perhaps a little
worried, Meg much the same but with a headache she can't understand. Her inability to remember the drum or the headache point
out again her ability not to see. Petey sounds much the same, but
one is a little hesitant to play him quite the same, given the
information we find him to have later in the act and the way he
decides to act upon it. He knows Stanley is unwell and though he
doesn't tell Meg, he will later momentarily stand against Goldberg
and McCann. Momentarily only, since though he sees more than
Meg does, he has no heroic strength that would allow him to act
upon what he sees. He will, finally, forget what he has seen and
see things as Meg sees them. Their last exchange is an ironic
comment on the importance to Petey of what he knows really
happened at the party the night before:

MEG   I was the belle of the ball.
PETEY   Were you?
MEG   Oh yes. They all said I was.
PETEY   I bet you were, too.
MEG   Oh, it's true. I was. [*Pause.*] I know I was.   [Act III]

The world is back to the way it can operate, blind and unknowing
or knowing but pretending to blindness. But the two important

scenes in the act, in relation both to the action of the play and to its demonstration of how language works, are Goldberg's collapse (of which I've already spoken) and our final look at Stanley. After Goldberg has looked at himself, shuddered, and recovered, he is ready for Stanley. Stanley arrives in McCann's hands manicured, marceled, dead. Again there is the question period, the inquisition, the test to see whether he can still attempt to fight with a meaningless world or whether he will accept it. His final "Uh-gugh . . . uh-gughh" let us know of his inability to argue against the world, and Goldberg's "Still the same old Stan" lets us know of his victory: the world of sound that hides the truth rather than a world which tries to reveal it is triumphant. Clearly the climax is this last interrogation.

This interrogation differs from its predecessor in two very real ways. First it is not really a series of questions to break Stanley down; the only questions really come at the end, after the verbal barrage, not during it. And second, the whole sequence from "Between you and me, Stan" to McCann's final "Animals" is not made up of questions definable or indefinable. Basically what Stanley is bombarded with are the joys of this world, of McCann's and Goldberg's world. He is told of what they will give him, and that is everything given us by movies, television, soap operas, commercials, billboards—in short, everything promised by the advertising agencies that want to sell us a life. Poor Stanley, like most of us in TV-land, is "myopic, anaemic, in a rut." Any of us could be on the other end of this commercial for the latest vitamin pill. So too the "free passes," the "season ticket," the "table reserved," the "hot tips" are that world promised us if we buy the right product, shop at the right discount house. Indeed if we go to the correct reducing salon, or use the right after-shave lotion, we too can become a "man," a "woman," be "reoriented," "rich," "adjusted." Of course, the point is made *in extremis,* but just barely. How close it is to the typical hard sell! And how close we all come to buying it, no matter how hard we say we couldn't care less! The danger for us is not that we might buy the recommended soap or gas or use the discount house, but our gradual conviction that the money saved, the look advertised, the life sold to us, is indeed worth having. I suspect most of us are more Meg or Petey in our awareness than Stanley. We live with it; Stanley gags on it.

This is Pinter's world in *The Birthday Party,* a world in which language, even gesture, hides truth (if truth there is), hides vulnerability, hides the possibility of connection. Glutted as we are in our life with words, Pinter moves us to recognition that the very glutting has deadened us. If, for example, Lulu is nothing but an animal—whose most open statement about her real interests is probably her remark to Stanley "You're a bit of a washout, aren't you?"—that which has kept her from being anything else are the deadening (because impersonal and merely conventional) convictions with which she tries to deal with that animal. Listen to her try to be shocked at Goldberg's dismissal of the sexual encounters of the night before:

LULU [*with growing anger*] You used me for a night. A passing fancy.
GOLDBERG Who used who?
LULU You made use of me by cunning when my defences were down.
GOLDBERG Who took them down?
LULU That's what you did. You quenched your ugly thirst. You took advantage of me when I was overwrought. I wouldn't do those things again, not even for a Sultan!
GOLDBERG One night doesn't make a harem.
LULU You taught me things a girl shouldn't know before she's been married at least three times!
GOLDBERG Now you're a jump ahead! What are you complaining about?

[*Enter* McCANN *quickly.*]

LULU You didn't appreciate me for myself. You took all those liberties only to satisfy your appetite.
GOLDBERG Now you're giving me indigestion. [Act III]

Oh, those horridly trite and overworked and unreal responses! How quickly we dismiss her shock as anything other than anger that Goldberg won't care about her! It is also interesting that Goldberg can afford to be straight with her, to answer her as he feels. He is probably more really "somebody" here than anywhere else in the play, though perhaps the important thing about him is not that he is ever anybody but simply that he supplies the correct response to what he hears to achieve his own ends—in this case, the dismissal of Lulu.

CHAPTER VI

VII

Conclusion: The Changing Use of Language in Drama

I have been interested and somewhat surprised in this look at language in drama not only in the ways the use of language changes but also in the direction those changes seem to point. What I find interesting, to my own surprise, is the way language seems to have progressively disappeared as meaningful. It is somehow clear when one reads Euripides (even in translation) and Shakespeare and Congreve that they believe in language. Even if they believe gradually less in its purity, they nonetheless believe. Euripides and Sophocles, it seems to me, speak with a view of a very simple, uncomplicated human psyche; that is, their heroes have basic problems, problems of how to cope with what happens to them or how to handle the force of the sexual drive or what constitutes human authority. Certainly these are the concerns of any serious play or playwright, but for the Greeks the problems are those happening to the best of general humanity, not to the interesting but unique specimens. There are no personalities as such in Greek tragedy, no manners. Their view is like the statue of the young *Charioteer* or the old *Zeus at Artemidorus,* not the *Laocoön* or the Hellenistic *Apollo.* We see a fairly straightforward view of the human being without particular personal problems. The human psyche is generalized, as is the human body depicted in the same period. The human figures in the friezes of the Parthenon are perfect human figures, not particular ones that we might know, from our own experience. The problems dealt with are general con-

135

cerns, concerns for the best of men, not for any particular variation of man. And the language reflects this generality. There is little indirection in speech. There are no Iagos here, saying one thing when they mean another. Characters mean what they say; we are not asked to consider, as we are in later drama, "What do they really mean?"

In Shakespeare, although we are still dealing with men who believe in language, we are also dealing with men who recognize its subtleties, its inadequacies. "What do you read, my lord?" "Words, words, words." Irony is now a dramatic concern. There is the recognition that truth, that ideal state, is difficult, perhaps impossible to find or pin down, and this realization becomes an important issue in drama. Part of the conflict in *Lear* or *Hamlet* is the search for real truth; it is the problem of digging under the surface lie of a Goneril or a Claudius. People lie in Shakespeare, and the discovery of those lies is often a central concern of the dramatic action. Words mean, but they may mean something quite different from what they appear to; they may cover truth rather than expose it. While Shakespeare doesn't distrust human discourse, he recognizes its dangers. It is still persuasive, but of what is at least a question. This is one of the reasons I think actors and directors search underneath his words for the "real" action they suggest. The human animal is now particular, diverse, mannered, and he is pictured in all of the particular poses suggested by the *Laocoön* and denied in the *Charioteer.*

Shakespeare, then, asks us to concern ourselves with more diverse, because more particular, problems than the Greek tragedians did. It would be presumptuous to attempt to trace that change without looking at the whole impact of history on Europe's growth or change, and certainly I cannot undertake a comprehensive examination in this space. But to look at only one aspect of that change, consider the way the tone of voice in drama shifts in its treatment of the impact on man of Christianity.

Drama is a strange creature in the Middle Ages, growing inside the church in its ritual, finally leaving the church in search of something more inclusive of human experience than a simplified symbolic representation of its difficulties. It gradually shapes itself in a more public arena that could allow both the symbolic reference and its exploitation. *Everyman,* for example, though not part of the church service, does not stray far from simple Christian convictions. The simple and unsophisticated search for meaning in life, and the final recognition that such meaning lay in a belief in God and the consequent possibility of eternal life, are expressed in terms that only the most confirmed and unquestioning believer in Christianity could recognize as a portrait of the human condition. There is no questioning of how God works here; indeed, there is only the most passing interest in any human interests except such recognizably limited ones as worldly goods and fellowship. Pride in one's own convictions and their efficacy, doubt about God's power or dominion, the anti-Christian drive of sex—these concepts are not even brought up in the play. It is a charming play, more propaganda than serious debate, but the very simplicity of the language allows the adjective "charming" rather than any more intense. It is a morality play, the avowed purpose of which is to teach us, and the voice speaking to us, though it is not without a certain irony, is basically a simple voice and speaks with an innocence and directness that seem applicable only to a very simple mind. The character presented is made aware suddenly that he must die, and in the face of this incontrovertible fact he finds that no one, that indeed nothing, except his faith in God's grace, can accompany him on that unknown journey, the possible end of which is eternal life. The conflicts in such an existence are only the recognition on the part of Everyman of his own stupidity in not seeing sooner that none of his worldly possessions could last forever:

DEATH   What, thinkest thou thy life is given thee,
  And thy worldly goods also?
EVERYMAN   I had thought so, verily.
DEATH   Nay, nay; it was but lent thee!
  For, as soon as thou art gone,
  Another a while shall have it, and then go therefrom
  Even as thou has done.
  Everyman, thou art mad! Thou hast thy wits five,
  And here on earth will not amend thy life;
  For suddenly I do come.

And Everyman admits as much. There is little real pain in his fears and no despair. Listen to him:

Alas, I may well weep with sighs deep.
Now have I no manner of company

To help me in my journey, and me to keep:
And also my writing is full unready.
What shall I do now for to excuse me?
I would to God I had never been begot!
To my soul a full great profit it would be;
For now I fear pains huge and great.

Now listen to Faustus in the next-to-last scene of Marlowe's play, written about a hundred years after *Everyman:*

Where art thou, Faustus? Wretch, what hast thou done!
Hell claims his right and with a roaring voice
Says "Faustus, come, thine hour is almost come!"
And Faustus now will come to do thee right.

To be sure, one can argue simply that Marlowe is a better poet than the anonymous author of *Everyman,* but that really ignores the crucial fact that Marlowe's Everyman is one tortured by a good deal more than his own stupidity and hell's pains. *Everyman's* concerns are general, nonspecific, and apparently only vaguely understood. He visualizes nothing, neither the joys of heaven nor the pains of hell, with the same imagination that Faustus does. Remember Faustus' last speech?

O, I'll leap up to Heaven! Who pulls me down?
(See, see, where Christ's blood streams in the firmament!)
One drop of blood will save me. O my Christ!
Rend not my heart for naming of my Christ!

And it is precisely this imagination that not only has let him see his loss, but indeed had suggested to him originally what his rejection of God might gain him. Both plays start from a Christian cloth, but Marlowe has poked dangerous holes in the whole fabric. He begins to question the earlier play's assumptions. His play has a conflict in its action that begins to concern other than confirmed Christians.

Man has come a long way in those hundred years, and his language lets us know it. But part of that journey suggests where he is apparently heading. In *Everyman* the universe and God and man's position in it are simple, explicable. In *Doctor Faustus,* the universe is confusing, man is uncomfortable with the discovery that he has a brain that a Christian God wants him to use only in pieces. By the time of *Lear,* man is unable to see with any clarity at all God's position in relation to man's morality:

LEAR What, art mad? A man may see how this world goes with no eyes. Look with thine ears: see how yon justice rails upon yond simple thief. Hark, in thine ear: change places; and, handy-dandy, which is the justice, which is the thief? Thou hast seen a farmer's dog bark at a beggar?

GLOUCESTER Ay, sir.

LEAR And the creature run from the cur? There thou mightst behold the great image of authority: a dog's obeyed in office. Thou rascal beadle, hold thy bloody hand!

> Why dost thou lash that whore: Strip thine own back;
> Thou hotly lust'st to use her in that kind
> For which thou whipp'st her. The usurer hangs the cozener.
> Through tatter'd clothes small vices do appear;
> Robes and furr'd gowns hide all. Plate sin with gold,
> And the strong lance of justice hurtless breaks;
> Arm it in rags, a pigmy's straw doth pierce it.
> None does offend, none, I say none; I'll able 'em:
> Take that of me, my friend, who have the power
> To seal the accuser's lips. Get thee glass eyes;
> And, like a scurvy politician, seem
> To see the things thou does not. Now, now, now, now;
> Pull off my boots: harder: harder, so.   [IV, 6]

Mad he may be, but it is also our madness. The inversion of morality is neither inexplicable nor outside our experience. At least with Edgar we must say, "O! matter and impertinency mix'd; / Reason in madness." Language has come far in articulating man's concerns, perhaps as far as it will ever come in English; but what it has at the same time let us see is the chaos we are trying to hold together. And part of the history of drama from now on is its verbal collapse, its inability to cope in any conclusive terms with that chaos. In tragedy only Webster can take us farther than this, and that's to the emotionally supported conviction that only death is real, that life's a joke.

I suppose the conviction is nowhere more moving than in the ironic song Bosola sings to the about-to-be-murdered Duchess of Malfi:

> Hark, now everything is still
> The screech-owl and the whistler shrill
> Call upon our dame aloud,
> And bid her quickly don her shroud!
> Much you had of land and rent;
> Your length in clay's now competent:
> A long war disturbed your mind;

> Here your perfect peace is signed.
> Of what is't fools make such vain keeping?
> Sin their conception, their birth weeping.
> Their life a general mist of error,
> Their death a hideous storm of terror.
> Strew your hair with powders sweet,
> Don clean linen, bathe your feet,
> And (the foul fiend more to check)
> A crucifix let bless your neck:
> 'Tis now full tide 'tween night and day;
> End your groan and come away.   [IV, 2]

What an uncomfortable, but persuasive view of the meaninglessness of life! But if this seems too much a set piece, a lyric poem, listen to Bosola at his own death, having just given a fatal thrust to the Cardinal:

> Yes, I hold my weary soul in my teeth;
> 'Tis ready to part from me. I do glory
> That thou, which stood'st like a huge pyramid
> Begun upon a large and ample base,
> Shalt end in a little point, a kind of nothing.   [V, 5]

That joke about the hole that has punctured the church is a comment on its worth as well as the Cardinal's. Even his own death is a joke. When asked how he came by it, he replies:

> In a mist; I know not how:
> Such a mistake as I have often seen
> In a play. O, I am gone!
> We are only like dead walls or vaulted graves,
> That ruined, yield no echo. Fare you well. [V, 5]

He tries to end it with a moral truth about the good fight, but it comes out like an aphorism. When this play is done correctly, with Ferdinand shrieking for wet hay like a sick horse as he dies, I think we see the real animal underneath that human exterior. It is Francis Bacon's view of El Greco's popes, not El Greco's. It is a horrifying view of mortality and of human worth that Webster gives us, but he uses words with great care to do it.

Tragedy, indeed serious drama, doesn't use words with the same trust again. Comedy does, if my reading of Congreve and Farquhar is right. Their cynicism is not so complete that it denies the precision of language in pointing out the animal limitations of man, his silliness; but by the late eighteenth and nineteenth centuries, even this is gone. Shaw is a kind of wonderful Edwardian outburst, perhaps as glorious and as ephemeral as the strange decade or so he represented—the last flicker before World War I. Hemingway defined the thoroughness of our distrust of words as well as anyone. Lieutenant Henry speaks for art as well as life in the world Hemingway saw in the 1920's:

I was always embarrassed by the words sacred, glorious, and sacrifice and the expression in vain. We had heard them, sometimes standing in the rain almost out of earshot, so that only the shouted words came through, and had read them, on proclamations that were slapped up by billposters over other proclamations, now for a long time, and I had seen nothing sacred, and the things that were glorious had no glory and the sacrifices were like the stockyards at Chicago if nothing was done with the meat except to bury it. There were many words that you could not stand to hear and finally only the names of places had dignity. Certain numbers were the same way and certain dates and these with the names of the places were all you could say and have them mean anything. Abstract words such as glory, honor, courage, or hallow were obscene beside the concrete names of villages, the numbers of roads, the names of rivers, the numbers of regiments and the dates.[1]

Words need reshaping, reuse, if they are to suggest a meaningful conviction like honor, or a ritual that could be termed either sacred or glorious. Chekhov had suggested as much a couple of decades earlier, when his plays showed us at once the need for verbal connection and the difficulty of achieving it in casual, conversational prose. Chekhov's "sacred" and "glorious" were Astrov's attempt to describe Russia's loss of her natural resources in *Uncle Vanya* or Petya's description of what Russia will become, in Act II of *The Cherry Orchard;* or even Olga's plea "we must work" as a meaningful answer at the end of *The Three Sisters.* The words, though obviously different words from Lieutenant Henry's, are still attempting to express man's needs, his desires and his ways of achieving them. Underneath that recognition of the difficulty of such connection, the pain of such loss, is the desire to find some way to get back to what is primal, real—indeed to get back to a new religious ritual, a new way to connect. Strindberg must have sensed something like the same inadequacy of language, at least language in its more conversational idiom. I assume it is part of the reason for his movement from *The Father* and its naturalistic counterparts

---

[1] Ernest Hemingway, *A Farewell to Arms* (Bantam Books, 1955), p. 137.

to *The Dream Play* and his almost hallucinatory search for God, for Indra.

I don't mean to suggest that this cursory outline of drama's change in at least the Christian world for the last five hundred years is in any way definitive. It rests, however, on one assumption that I think is essential to any artistic endeavor, theatre included; namely, art attempts to help man see what he is and helps him to shape those insights into something he can live with. To understand the human condition is nothing more than such an attempt, whether it is spoken of in terms of God and original sin or id, ego, and superego. One's attempt in any art form is to suggest that condition and a way to cope with it. Words or colors, shapes or sounds are the raw material with which we try to shape our insights, our reactions to our own humanity. The theatre has the unique advantage of using all these materials in its own attempt to return to connection. At the moment, it seems to me, words are being given short shrift by many playwrights. It is as though they had lost their belief in the grammar that shapes words' meaning. Ginsberg often writes this way, as if the main means of communication were sound and connotation, undefined by any context or grammar. Words are used to point, but only generally. Artaud—when I understand him at all—seems to want a preverbal, inexplicable conflagration on the stage that will unite observers with performers unhampered by definition, by what it means. While I can understand the need for art to move one, it also seems to me important that that emotional response have within it at least the seeds of definition. Connection's value, after all, is that it can happen in some way other than an accidental way.

What I think is important here is that the attempt to create response in an audience is moving away from verbal appeal. Even those who use words, and are at the same time influential in theatre's growth, often use them in a general rather than a personal way. Brecht, for example, is concerned with the political and hence general issues that define the human condition, not the personal. Words are generalized pointers not precise definers. As I understand Shen Te-Shui ta in *The Good Woman of Setzuan* or Grusha in *The Caucasian Chalk Circle,* they both seem to me attitudes examined under a general social pressure rather than a personal psychological one. I recognize that the two categories need not be mutually exclusive, but it is more and more difficult to understand modern drama in both camps at once. While it seems to me possible to read Pinter's *The Birthday Party* as an ironic denunciation of the limitations of an "efficiency-oriented value system" (as a politically minded colleague of mine would have it), it is only possible by looking at the general structure of the play and not listening to the particular way characters speak. So, too, I have heard analyses of Shen Te-Shui ta in terms of the two sides of "every personal psyche," but nothing in the translations I have read supports that "every" in more particular terms than "those oppressed by economic necessity." It has always seemed to me, in fact, that one of the clearest causes of Brecht's failure in production in this country (despite critical value judgments to the contrary) is our inability to understand the "pressures of economic necessity" in any immediate way. Even *Mother Courage,* which is for me the most moving of Brecht's major plays, is hard for us to understand on Brecht's terms. He apparently wanted us to scorn Mother Courage for her opportunism; I find her comparable to Hecuba in Euripides' *The Trojan Women* simply in her ability to keep living rather than quitting. But that, I take it, is my misreading, not Brecht's intention.

But this topic is perhaps the germ of another book. It is true, I think, that language in its more traditional grammar is proving inadequate, perhaps because the human experience it is attempting to cope with is continually bursting its traditional bounds. Rochelle Owens' *Futz* or Sam Shepard's *La Turista* seem to me incomplete and sketchy, but they are both fascinated with what language can do in the theatre. The critic can only hope that such fascination will find actors and directors who will help to articulate more clearly the action such playwrights have in mind. Actors and playwrights necessarily feed each other. New styles of acting allow new combinations of words, just as new combinations of words force new acting styles. I know absolutely no Polish, but I can't help feeling that Grotowski's company, if the television presentation of his *Acropolis* is a true reflection of his work, has discovered for itself not only a new vocabulary but a whole new acting style with which to present it. The essentially clumsy, obscene cloddishness of the acting (I don't use any of these words pejoratively) was, I hope, some kind of comment on the long lyric passages that were sung or spoken. To project the sense of selfishness, of survival at any cost, that I saw in the play demanded and received a new kind of acting, at least a far cry from the extended psychological investigation that has become such a trademark in American acting.

Because language is as important as the visual elements in the theatre, a close examination of it can tell an actor things about the way of delineating the action the playwright has given him. Chekhov's brilliance, whose lead Pinter has followed, has infected us so with subtext, with the action underneath the apparently discursive and meaningless surface, that the actor need not attend to that surface. The author's genius is his hiding of the event, and the actor's job is to rediscover it. Earlier playwrights exposed the action, and their genius was the careful delineation of it with language. The actor's job was necessarily to understand and project that language, indeed to find its hidden nuances. In modern drama, it is not that action has become unimportant, but that it has become hidden; the vital nuance now is its discovery. What past event has brought Goldberg to ferret out Stanley? Why is Stanley immediately fearful of that arrival? Since Pinter doesn't tell us, it becomes the actor's job to create that event for himself and by indirection for the audience, since only some event, however imaginary, will allow the actor to deliver Pinter's lines with conviction. So, too, in *The Three Sisters,* at what point in those "Tara-tara-taras" and "Tum-tums" of Masha and Vershinnin in Act III is their assignation made? Like Pinter, Chekhov leaves the decision to the actor; the moment is not spelled out.

I think this hiding of the action is about at an end. I frankly can't see anywhere else to hide it. If I am right, language will necessarily emerge again as a vital theatrical force, different certainly from what it was in Shakespeare's hands or Sophocles', but different also from what it has been for Chekhov and Pinter. Obviously it is the playwrights who will show its new direction to us, but I think as audience, as actor, and as director, we can help prepare the way by being alive to its potential. In our concern with image, we have tended perhaps to overlook language, to hear its clichés too often. We have tended not to trust it, because we hear it used with care so little. But if theatre, like any art, is to touch us, to shape our lives, it must use all its tools. That hint at *why* we suffer or enjoy, cry or laugh, is art's particular province. The answer to the question need not be conclusive or final, but the possibility of some kind of answer, no matter how far-fetched, is one of the things that keeps us alive. If there were no hope of such a possibility, even such a tentative one as Didi's activity persuades us to in *Waiting for Godot,* we would die, either willfully or unknowingly. Our life is an attempt to "trace the lineaments of experience on the face of concern," to understand it, not because we are critics or scholars or artists, but because "what concerns us is naturally an object of study," and our lives and what affects our lives fall into such a category.[2] Plays are such attempts, as are poems, symphonies, and paintings; and if plays are to be as moving as they can be, they need not only the careful use of sound and color and movement, but the careful use of words as well.

[2] The two quotations in this sentence are from J. V. Cunningham's defense of historical scholarship in the introduction to his book *Woe or Wonder* (University of Denver Press, 1951). The full introduction is not quite to the point here, but it is certainly the most intelligent and moving defense of the subject I know.

Bibliographical Essay

This section is aptly titled; it is an essay in that I have tried simply to list those works or talk about the translations of the plays themselves that have excited me or, in some cases, confused me. The bibliography is in no way comprehensive. Indeed, it is not even selective, since selectivity implies some kind of examination of the field under consideration and then intelligent choice. I think the comments about the works might be suggestive to the reader who is interested in pursuing the problems and joys of producing a play or visualizing a production of a play. The books mentioned and the accompanying comments are limited to works connected to those areas I have been most concerned with in the body of this volume.

GREEK TRAGEDY

AESCHYLUS. Though I have not talked about Aeschylus in the text, I think he is the playwright who among the Greeks is most apt to take our imaginations—if we can get some workable translations, and by "workable" I mean on the simplest level *speakable*. I have seen and read Philip Vellacott's translation of *Prometheus Bound,* for example, and it was as difficult to follow in production as it was unspeakable in the reading. Robert Lowell's translation, or adaptation, of the play (Farrar, Straus & Giroux, 1969) is an example of precisely the other extreme. It is clear, readable—in fact, a very exciting play—but it is no longer Aeschylus, or even Greek, in form. The chorus in the Lowell is three voices, and Prometheus is a highly articulate speaker for a change. These features make the play very stimulating, but it loses what I think will make Aeschylus finally most taking, namely, the ritual. How one can hold onto the simple action that will allow ritual and at the same time attend to the sophistication of Aeschylean verse, I don't know, but this is what must be done if Aeschylus is to be treated fairly.

The only translation that I know of at the moment which seems to manage both is one that I have seen only in manuscript: Helen

Bacon and Anthony Hecht's *The Seven Against Thebes*. These translators continually label possible ritual dances without removing them from the action of the play. Much which is simply talk in a translation like Grene's (David Grene and Richmond Lattimore, eds., *The Complete Greek Tragedies: Aeschylus II,* Washington Square Press, 1967) is visualized in the Bacon and Hecht. Odes are in the service of something: "a hymn to Hades," a dance with words, "the rape of the city," "a funeral ode," and so on. Yet the central issue of conflict between the women of Thebes and Eteocles and its resolution are never lost. It is because of this translation that I am hesitant in recommending the Grene-Lattimore series; still, it is better than the Oates and O'Neill (W. J. Oates and Eugene O'Neill, eds., *Complete Greek Drama,* 2 vols.; Random House, 1938) .

It should be noted that the Grene-Lattimore edition is in at least three different series of publications: (1) There is the three-volume set published by the University of Chicago Press in hard cover. (2) There is an earlier publication of the plays in hard back by the same publishers. This is in eight volumes: two of Aeschylus, two of Sophocles, and four of Euripides. This set was later reprinted in paperback form. (3) There is a new paperback series of the same plays put out by Washington Square Press with the permission of the University of Chicago Press. This last is also in eight volumes and though less sturdy than the paperback edition by the University of Chicago, it is less expensive.

SOPHOCLES. My own choice for both *Antigone* and *Oedipus Rex* is the Dudley Fitts translation, despite the loss in the former of Antigone's cold dismissal of a live Haemon in favor of her dead kin. Both plays are in *The Oedipus Cycle* (Dudley Fitts and Robert Fitzgerald, trans., Harvest Book, Harcourt, Brace, 1939) . The Kitto version of *Antigone* is worth consideration particularly if one is interested in a more formal production of the play. It is certainly readable, but I find it a little too distant. The formality of the verse tends to keep me away from the play. It appears in *Sophocles' Three Tragedies* (H. D. F. Kitto, trans., Oxford University Press, 1962) . The only modern translation of the *Ajax* that I know of is that of John Moore in the Grene-Lattimore series. It is, I am told, accurate; and it is playable. Moore, however, is not as good a poet as Fitts, and it is hard to believe, as a colleague of mine insists, that

Ajax's presuicide speech is one of the most moving speeches in all of Greek tragedy. The *Philoctetes* is playable in the Grene-Lattimore series, but Sophocles doesn't sound the poet he does in Fitts or indeed in the really fine translation of *Oedipus at Colonus* by Robert Fitzgerald. This translation appears not only in the Grene-Lattimore series, but also in *The Oedipus Cycle* mentioned above. The other plays of Sophocles I simply don't know well enough to comment on.

From my own experience I would recommend the Grene-Lattimore editions generally for all three Greek tragedians, though I should mention here—and again I am speaking from the convictions of colleagues who know Greek—that in any translation of Sophocles by R. C. Jebb (and he is the major translator in the Oates–O'Neill edition), one is apt to have the most exact translation if not always the most poetic or playable. He is a good man to trust when other translations are contradictory or simply unclear.

EURIPIDES. In some ways Grene and Lattimore are best served for Euripides, in having both Arrowsmith and Lattimore working for them. Arrowsmith translates *Orestes, The Bacchae, Heracles, Hecuba,* and *The Cyclops.* I have seen all of these plays produced except the *Hecuba,* and in fact have worked intimately with *The Bacchae, Heracles,* and *The Cyclops.* They are all three wonderfully speakable and playable. *The Cyclops* particularly deserves attention. Whatever a satyr play was, if this is a fair example of it, it was indeed something excitingly different in tone and intention from either Greek tragedy or Greek comedy. Lattimore translates *The Trojan Women* and *Alcestis* in the series. I have trouble with *Alcestis* as a play, but certainly the translation is not at fault, and *The Trojan Women* is a beautiful translation, I think. For people interested in exploring Euripides I suggest starting with *The Trojan Women* and *The Bacchae* rather than with *Medea* and *Hippolytus.* Professional and even college productions suggest that interested producers already have attended to the former two plays, but I am surprised at how often beginning students know only the latter two.

SECONDARY SOURCES. The works mentioned here are those which have helped me begin my own researches in producing a play and at the same time have some relation to Greek tragedy. H. D. F. Kitto's book *Greek Tragedy* (3rd ed.; Methuen, 1961) is an excellent beginning. He has an essay on every tragedy in the canon, and whether or not one agrees, he generally presents a point of view about each. He has also written a little book called *The Greeks* (Penguin Books, 1951), in which one is given some idea of the world out of which these playwrights came. I think the greatest help are individual studies of the plays at length. Two exceptional ones come to mind on *Oedipus Rex* and *The Bacchae:* Bernard Knox, *Oedipus at Thebes* (Yale University Press, 1957); and R. P. Winnington-Ingram, *Euripides and Dionysus* (Cambridge University Press, 1948).

General studies of the three major playwrights are: H. W. Smyth, *Aeschylean Tragedy* (University of California Press, 1924); C. N. Whitman, *Sophocles, a Study of Heroic Humanism* (Harvard University Press, 1951); and C. M. A. Grube, *Drama of Euripides* (Methuen, 1941; reprinted 1961). Grube's book is not at all outstanding, but it does talk about all the plays, and his concerns are of the way they work. The Smyth is the only book I know of that is helpful in understanding Aeschylean plays. For Sophocles, Whitman is a good beginning but, like most writers on Sophocles, Whitman makes him too easy. Sometimes work like that of Gilbert Murray, though at the moment much discredited, is very suggestive. His theory of the "year-spirit" was first elucidated, according to Gerard Else in his *The Origin and Early Form of Greek Tragedy* (Harvard University Press, 1967), in Jane Harrison's *Themis* (Cambridge University Press, 1912), in an essay by Murray (pp. 341–363) entitled "Excursus on the Ritual Forms Preserved in Greek Tragedy," now available in paperback. The value of the essay is not its accuracy—Sir Arthur Pickard-Cambridge has pretty well destroyed it in *Dithyramb, Tragedy and Comedy* (Oxford University Press, 1927)—but in its suggestiveness. There are ritualistic sections in Greek tragedy, at least the language suggests as much, and Murray gives a producer possible ritual frames. Such apparently muddleheaded brilliance is often more helpful than Pickard-Cambridge's deadly clearheaded assurances that we can know nothing at all.

And finally structural analyses like Aristotle's in his *Poetics* and Else's in his *The Origin and Early Form of Greek Tragedy* referred to above seem to me invaluable in reminding one not only of the need for some organizing principle to hold a production together, but of those principles of organization that are drawn directly from the plays being looked at. Though there are many translations of the *Poetics,* I recommend Else's (Harvard University Press, 1963). His commentary is brilliant.

SHAKESPEARE

Bibliographical material on Shakespeare is so immense that it is impossible to survey it without a much fuller knowledge than I possess of what is available. What I should like to do is suggest the kinds of studies that have helped me—which is not to say that much I won't mention hasn't also been helpful. Clearly, books like Theodore Spencer's *Shakespeare and the Nature of Man* (Macmillan, 1942) or E. M. W. Tillyard's *Elizabethan World Picture* (Macmillan, 1944) are helpful in familiarizing oneself with the philosophical views which often concerned Shakespeare. The danger of such books is that they may lead one away from the play and toward a moral tract (unless one is careful), but they are still helpful. Anything that helps one see the period may well help one see the play. So too, source studies like Tillyard's *Shakespeare's History Plays* (Macmillan, 1946) are helpful in finding out what Shakespeare started from, but they are not of immediate value in telling one where to go. Studies like Caroline Spurgeon's *Shakespeare's Imagery and What It Tells Us* (Cambridge University Press, 1952) is not of much value to an actor looking for motives. This is not to say that it might not be very helpful to a designer who is looking for a way to visualize the play.

My own bias is clearly toward that which helps me see the action of the play, that helps tell the story. I suppose in this sense I am inevitably and finally an Aristotelian, however dangerous the implications of that label may be. My favorite critic is Granville-Barker. I think his *Prefaces to Shakespeare* (Princeton University Press, 1946) the most rewarding book I have read on the plays it deals with. I find even such wonderfully extreme books—that is, extreme in looking for what goes on in a play—as J. Dover Wilson's *What Happens in Hamlet* (Cambridge University Press, 1960, finally a paperback edition) exceptionally helpful. I would like to see all the tragedies looked at in the same way. It is probably my Aristotelian bias that makes me look with such favor on A. C. Bradley's *Shakespearean Tragedy* (Macmillan, 1951), although frankly it is not Bradley's analysis of action which I find most helpful, but his attention to the psychology of his characters. I suspect that as long as actors lean on the psychology of the characters they play, as American actors do, he will be valuable. And finally a suggestive, if often insane, critic is Jan Kott in his *Shakespeare, Our Contemporary*, now in paperback (Anchor Books, Doubleday). He is worth any director's attention if only to be dismissed.

As to texts, I find the Arden editions the best for all the plays (published by Methuen and by Harvard University Press from 1899 to the present). The general editors of the Arden editions have been W. J. Craig (1899–1906), R. H. Case (1909–1944), Una Ellis-Fermor (1946–1958), and at present Harold F. Brooks and Harold Jenkins. Perhaps it is the continuity of the editors' concern and their continuous attention to new scholarship which make the Arden editions by far the most thorough. They are not in paper and they are not inexpensive but I would still recommend them. There are some particular editions that I think are of particular and rather different interest. Bertram Josephs has edited *Lear* in *The London English Literature Series* (G. C. Rosser, ed., University of London Press, 1966). Mr. Josephs' concern is keeping always before us the event that the characters are discussing. Hence his gloss gives those readings that the context of the play suggests rather than the most obvious, noncontextual paraphrase one might give. It makes for very close reading of the text, but it is often very rewarding.

The one other direction of Shakespearean criticism I would like to see expanded is the kind of thing Charles Shattuck has done with Macready's productions of *As You Like It* and *King John*. The first was published as *Macready's As You Like It* (Urbana, Ill.: Beta Phi Mu, 1962); the latter as *Macready's King John* (University of Illinois Press, 1962). Basically they are recreated prompt books with the notes on costumes and sets of Macready's productions of the plays. Since we are always part of a tradition in producing Shakespeare, I get not only encouragement in finding that Macready,

Booth, Garrick, or Forbes-Robertson faced many of the same problems I must face, but obvious assistance from their solutions. Unfortunately, my information on Booth and Garrick is either hearsay or scattered references. I could wish their productions were as thoroughly documented as these two of Macready's. I think, in this regard, it is informative to look at the French edition of *Hamlet* which still uses the Forbes-Robertson production as its text, with illustrations and cuts. It is informative not only to understand Forbes-Robertson or the theatre of 1920, but *Hamlet* as well. This kind of examination can be seen in its most general outline in what may be the seminal work in this kind of study, A. C. Sprague's *Shakespeare and the Actors* (Harvard University Press, 1944). Sprague's bibliography is extensive and his notes informative. He is fascinating to read just to rediscover stage business done by famous actors, but his quotations also remind us of the problems one must continually face in producing Shakespeare. Stage business as used by famous actors, the ostensible subject of the book, reaches much further than simple description; that is, the description often suggests a whole interpretation. Sprague's work also reminds one of the truly great critics of Shakespearean acting. One immediately thinks of George Bernard Shaw on Henry Irving (John F. Matthews, ed., *Shaw's Dramatic Criticism,* Hill and Wang, 1959) or of William Hazlitt (William Archer and Robert Lowe, eds., *Hazlitt on Theatre,* Hill and Wang, n.d.) and George Henry Lewes (*On Actors and the Art of Acting,* Evergreen Books, Grove Press, n.d.) on Edmund Kean's interpretations. All three of these books are available in paperback—Shaw in selected form, Hazlitt and Lewes fairly completely.

Finally I would recommend for producers of Shakespeare, John Russell Brown, *Shakespeare's Plays in Performance* (St. Martin's Press, 1967). Brown is an able critic, and the aims in his introduction parallel my own. His approach is not mine, but his concerns certainly are, as his introduction suggests. I quote the first two paragraphs:

Why are Shakespeare's plays so actable? How do they draw and hold their audiences? How can we gain an impression of performance from reading a text? How should the plays be staged in our theatres to present the fullness of Shakespeare's imagination? These are some of the questions that led me to write this book, to try one approach and then another, to experiment in stage-productions and in research and argument. A knowledge of what precisely can and should happen when a play is performed is, for me, the essential first step towards an understanding of Shakespeare, and perhaps the most difficult and fascinating of all.

I start with the text and the actor, which is the closest point of contact between Shakespeare and those who perform his plays. Problems of style and interpretation are at once encountered, and confusions due to changes in taste and conditions of performance. While general considerations prepare for the more particular, every chapter in the first part of the book is basically concerned with how an actor must respond to the text and what reevaluations of that text are accomplished by his performance. I have tried to look and listen, as well as read, to respond to entire characterizations as well as momentary and immediate effects, and to remember the excitement of great and original performances.

RESTORATION AND EIGHTEENTH-CENTURY COMEDY

The Restoration and eighteenth-century comedies talked about in this book have only recently been receiving much attention, so it may be helpful to give some general histories of the plays and periods. The best-known are G. H. Nettleton, *English Drama of the Restoration and 18th Century* (Macmillan, 1914); Allardyce Nicoll, *The Restoration Drama* and *Early 18th Century Drama*, Vols. 1 and 2 of Nicoll's *History of English Drama, 1660–1900* (Cambridge University Press).

For a general treatment of the plays themselves, I suppose T. H. Fujimura's *Restoration Comedy of Wit* (Princeton University Press, 1952) is still the most helpful. There are three other books which are more particular in their attention: Norman Holland, *The First Modern Comedies* (Harvard University Press, 1959); Dale Underwood, *Etherege and the Seventeenth Century Comedy of Manners* (Yale University Press, 1957); and Paul and Miriam Mueschke, *New View of Congreve's Way of the World* (University of Michigan Press, 1958). All of these books can be helpful, but none of them is really concerned with the plays as plays. Fujimura is helpful in picturing for us some of the aspects of the central couple, and the other three do give readings of the plays. One can get some idea of the approaches of Underwood and Holland in a paperback collection of essays edited by John Loftis and entitled *Restoration Drama, Modern Essays in Criticism* (Oxford University Press, 1966). Selections from their books listed above are reprinted. One can also find here L. C. Knight's famous essay denouncing Restoration drama as simply bad literature. It is entitled "Restoration Comedy: the Reality and the Myth" and was originally published in *Explorations: Essays in Criticism Mainly of the Literature of the Seventeenth Century* (Chatto and Windus, 1946).

Since Bonamy Dobree in *Restoration Comedy* (Oxford University Press, 1924) and Joseph Wood Krutch in *Comedy and Conscience in the Restoration* (Columbia University Press, 1924) reestablished the possibility at least of the morality of Restoration comedies, criticism since has been perhaps too concerned with the stance these writers have taken and not enough concerned with how they made that stance compelling. The Loftis volume, mentioned above, is a good sampling of such criticism. There are, I think, more compelling essays in the fairly new paperback edited by J. R. Brown and Bernard Harris, *Restoration Theatre* (Capricorn Books, Putnam, 1967). There is a fine essay by Anne Righter on Wycherley. Her reading of *The Country Wife* suggests what is sloppy in Holland's reading. So too Muir's reading of *The Country Wife* is more perceptive than Mueschke's. Also in this volume there is a short but helpful bibliography for every author discussed.

The eighteenth century doesn't fare as well as the seventeenth in discussion of its comic dramatists. There are studies of sentimentalism, but for the most part they only prove the impossibility of doing most eighteenth-century comedy until we come to Sheridan and Goldsmith. For a general outline of the growth of sentimentality and how it operates in plays, Ernest Bernbaum's *Drama of Sensibility* (Ginn, 1915) is excellent, but it doesn't give us many producible plays. Goldsmith, probably because he is a playmaker, is harder to talk about as a writer. Sheridan has received some attention, but the best of it seems to find him a writer who says little but says it brilliantly. For what is worthwhile from such attention, I recommend Louis Kronenberger's introduction to *The School for Scandal* mentioned in the Foreword. I fear I am guilty of the same kind of criticism in my own introduction to the play (Chandler Publishing Company, 1961). Perhaps the best of such criticism is a little-known volume by the English critic William A. Darlington, entitled simply *Sheridan* (British Book Center, 1951).

Texts for those playwrights I think of as particularly producible—Etherege, Wycherley, Congreve, Farquhar, Vanbrugh, Goldsmith, and Sheridan—are available in the Mermaid Dramabook Series reprinted from the old hard-cover Mermaid editions, except for Etherege and Vanbrugh. Vanbrugh is available in the Mermaid edition listed in the Foreword. Etherege, as far as I know, is only available complete in his *Dramatic Works* (H. F. B. Brett-Smith, ed., Blackwell, 1927).

CHEKHOV

The greatest service I can think of, to producers of Chekhov, is to have him continually translated. The list—from Garnett to Dunnigan—is endless, but each translation helps one see more. In choosing Elizaveta Fen's *The Three Sisters*, I was at once choosing what to me was a fairly modern translation without being contemporary. I looked at the time at Ann Dunningan's translation in *Chekhov: The Major Plays* (Signet Classic, New American Library, 1964), which I had been told was particularly readable and playable. Indeed it is—for me, a little too much so. It is worth looking at for any producer of the play, but for me it pushed the early twentieth century out of focus, and I was hearing, almost to embarrassment, my immediate contemporary world. It was somehow Chekhov in modern dress. My own favorite single translation, despite the Englishness of its idiom is David Magarshack's translation of *The Seagull*. Magarshack has now translated the major plays in *Anton Chekhov: Four Plays* (Hill and Wang, 1969).

What I have found most helpful in trying to understand Chekhov is everything he says. As a consequence I would recommend the following books as a means of hearing him talk to people:

Letters of Anton Tchekhov to Olga Knipper (Constance Garnett, ed., Blom, 1966)
Life and Letters of Anton Tchekhov (S. S. Koteliansky and Philip Tomlinson, eds., Blom, 1965)
Notebook of Anton Tchekhov (S. S. Koteliansky and Leonard Woolf, trans., Huebsch, 1921)
Chekhov: A Life (David Magarshack, Evergreen Books, Grove Press, 1955)
Chekhov the Dramatist (David Magarshack, Hill and Wang, 1960)

Chekhov: A Biographical and Critical Study by Ronald Hingley
(Barnes and Noble, 1966)

1860–1960 A. P. Chekhov (Julius Katzer, ed., Foreign Languages
Publishing House, n.d.)

The letters are of interest as comment on Chekhov's whole view of
the human condition, but the correspondence with Olga Knipper
has some immediate comment on roles she played, such as Masha in
The Three Sisters and Madame Ranavskaya in *The Cherry
Orchard*. The Magarshack studies, though of some critical interest,
are of equal interest in the great amount of Chekhov quoted in
both books.

Modern criticism as such is abundant. I would recommend the
following:

A. Ganz, "Arrivals and Departures: The Meaning of the Journey in
the Major Plays of Chekhov," *Drama Survey,* Vol. 5 (Spring
1966), pp. 5–23. This is one of the few studies that concentrate
on the very central action of his plays.

J. L. Styan, *The Dark Comedy* (Cambridge University Press, 1962).
A very careful analysis; perhaps it catches me because it is so
unlike my own enthusiasms.

Maurice Valency, *The Breaking String* (Oxford University Press,
1966). The introductory chapter is on the Russian theatre.

Robert Brustein, *The Theatre of Revolt* (Little, Brown, 1962). I
don't like Brustein's view of Chekhov, but it is helpful in
putting the playwright against his contemporaries.

"Chekhov Centenary," *World Theatre,* Vol. 9 (Summer 1960), pp.
99–148. Pictures of his productions throughout the world.

PINTER

Bibliography on Pinter is, in my case, pretty meaningless; I simply
don't know any works on him. I mentioned the Dukore article in
the text, and there is another in the same issue of the *Tulane
Drama Review* (March, 1962), by Ruby Cohen, entitled "The
World of Harold Pinter." But these are the only things that I have
read about him except in the two standard books on the avant-
garde of the past fifteen years: Martin Esslin, *Theatre of the Absurd*

(Anchor Books, Doubleday, 1961); and J. R. Taylor, *The Angry Theatre* (Hill and Wang, 1962), entitled *Anger and After* in its British publication. Clearly, these books knew only about Pinter's beginnings; they can do little more than mention him, but they are a start. I have been most taken by what he himself has said in newspaper interviews or personal interviews, but with the exception of the piece quoted in the text I have no references to other interviews.

Index